WORKING FROM
HOME
EFFECTIVELY

JOE MARKLEY

DEDICATION.

To the working man:

Contrary to what Sonny from "A Bronx Tale" says, he's not a sucker if he works from home.

CONTENTS

INTRODUCTION

PART 1

MY REMOTE WORK STORY: HOW I EVOLVED FROM A CORPORATE DRONE TO A WORK-AT-HOME SUPERSTAR

PART 2

TYPES OF WORK YOU CAN DO FROM HOME

PART 3

"BEST" PRACTICES AND ROUTINES YOU CAN USE TO WORK
FROM HOME EFFECTIVELY

PART 4

NON-OBVIOUS BENEFITS OF WORKING FROM HOME

PART 5

TIPS, TRICKS & TRAPS TO WORK FROM HOME EFFECTIVELY

INTRODUCTION

WORKING FROM HOME: WHY IT'S BETTER

BOSS: "I'm going to get right to the point. It has come to my attention that you and the cleaning woman have engaged in sexual intercourse on the desk in your office. Is that correct?"

GEORGE: "Who said that?"

BOSS: "She did."

GEORGE: "Was that wrong?"

SEINFELD: THE RED DOT, EPISODE 29

orking in an office is a *pain*. You lose a significant portion of your day to commute time and then, when you get to the office, you have to deal with being in the office. This means you have to deal with the office politics. You have to deal with the person who interrupts your train of thought when you're trying to figure out a complicated problem. And usually the interruption is for superficial topics like, "what are you doing after work?" or "what's for lunch?" or "do you want to go get a coffee?" or "do you want to go get a beer?" You get the idea.

The office also has a stifling aroma. You have the person who brings the smelly lunch (read: tuna fish sandwich). Or the person who makes popcorn in the kitchen microwave, and that popcorn smell wafts through the office like a siren. Then there's the person who has the smelly feet and always takes his shoes off (and this person is always a male), and the close-talker who has the smelly breath. Offices can be smelly, disgusting cesspools.

If you can avoid being in the office as much as possible, all while excelling at your job and ensuring your boss and others know you're excelling at your job, you will always be ahead of the game.

Working from home provides you with the ultimate flexibility. You can start work when you want – many times much earlier than you would if you had to deal with a commute. You can take breaks when you want to take breaks. You can finish your day when you want to finish. You can plan your meals to optimize your daily nutrition and your performance throughout the day. You can conserve your energy for the truly difficult tasks associated with your job. In short, you have control over your day.

Here are just three of many reasons why working from home is a better option than working in the office full-time: time savings, cost savings, and creativity-killing office culture.

INTRODUCTION

TIME SAVINGS — YOU'RE WORTH IT

You lose a substantial amount of your day commuting – I know some people who commute 2+ hours each way to the office. That's 4-5 hours per day, or 20-25 hours per week. That's almost another job. What a horrible way to spend your waking hours.

You don't have to be a math major to see just how much your time is lost to commuting, and what that could mean for you in terms of dollars. Here is a back-of-the-envelope example: let's say your time is worth $100 per hour. For some people that may seem like a big number. For others it may actually be a little low, but for our purposes we'll use $100 per hour as a rough guide. You may compute your own results differently based on a different rate.

How did I come up with $100 per hour? Let's say you make $60,000 per year. That breaks down to roughly $29 per hour in gross earnings if you're working a 40-hour week. But this isn't your true cost per hour. Let's say your employer provides typical employee benefits – those amount to 50% or so of your salary. So that's $14 per hour in benefits, and $43 per hour total. Also, you're providing value to your company. You're producing revenue, or reducing costs, or producing goods to sell, or ensuring goods are of high quality, etc. That value is worth something to your employer.

If you think of your value to your employer in geeky baseball terms, think of it like the WAR, or the "win above replacement player." The WAR is a relatively new stat that baseball's saber-metric fanatics use to gauge a player's value. The higher the WAR, the better the player is compared to an average player.

You will know if you're a good employee – let's say you have above average annual reviews, you're in the top quintile of sales reps, you've gotten some employee recognition awards, etc. If you're a good employee, your "WAR" is higher than 1X your salary and benefits cost – in some cases it could be 2X or 3X or even higher. Otherwise, it wouldn't be profitable for your employer to keep you on the books. So for our example, let's say that you are producing 25% more than your cost – which is a relatively low percentage. Given that conservative 25% production, that would mean your employee WAR is $54.

Again, you can use this calculation method as a guide and

change the parameters as much as you see fit. You may be a sales rep and know with certainty that your WAR is 3 times higher than your cost. If that's the case, your total value per hour will be much higher, and this example will ring even truer for you.

So that's $43 of cost plus $54 in WAR equals $97 per hour – I'm rounding up to $100 per hour to make the math easier. Let's say also that your average one-way commute is 30 minutes. This is a few minutes more than the national average based on a study done by the Population Reference Bureau in September 2014. Their calculation was 26 minutes. But for simplicity and for easy math, let's use 30 minutes.

So for an hour per day, you're wasting $100 in total value by commuting. Adding that up for the year, if you work 5 days per week for 50 weeks (assume 2 weeks' vacation), then that's $25,000 per year you're wasting by commuting. And that's if you make $60,000. So that's 42% of your annual salary you're wasting on commuting.

Quite simply, commuting does not add up. Mathematically it's a losing trade, both for the employee, who's wasting 5 hours per week on average getting to & from the office, and the employer, who's losing 5 productive hours per week of that same employee worth $100 per hour.

Additionally, and this is less quantitative, you have the issue of employee morale and energy level, or ability to focus. After a

30-minute commute, which sometimes can be stressful (traffic, spilled coffee, belligerent sports talk show host bashing your favorite player), often times workers need a few minutes to get "settled" at the office.

So the first 30 minutes or so of their office day may be somewhat wasted, too. If an employee isn't in the right mindset to work effectively, she will not work effectively. In the words of "Cool Hand" Luke: "I got my mind right." With a right mind, you can face the task at hand, whatever that task may be. But if you come into the office frustrated, or frazzled, or stressed from your morning commute, you may not be ready for real work right away. This not only robs the employee of peak productivity time (between 2 and 4 hours after waking up), but also robs the employer of that same time. It's a lose-lose.

We weren't made to sit in traffic. Or to deal with faulty bus air conditioning or fighting over space on a subway. We were made to move, to create, to act, and to think. We should focus our attention on doing those things, and not on all the distractions that come along with the daily commute. By working from home, you can cut out all the noise and focus on the good stuff.

INTRODUCTION

MONEY SAVINGS

Time isn't the only thing you save by avoiding the daily commute and working from home. Getting to and from work costs money! You may not think about it too much because you are so used to paying for the means of getting back and forth to work. But it is a cost you can eliminate.

Think about how you get to work today. You may drive into the office. If you do that, you're putting miles on your car, which leads to more gasoline, more oil changes, more maintenance, brake changes, tire replacements, and eventually a new car. If you didn't have the daily commute, you may still have a car, but you wouldn't be putting on nearly as many miles, saving the car and your wallet a significant cost. This could be a savings of several hundred or even thousands of dollars per year.

Also, you may be running late to the office in the morning. Many times this is probably the case, because you didn't get adequate sleep and you have to wake up early to beat the traffic into work. You make a stop at Dunkin' Donuts and grab a bagel sandwich and a large coffee – most likely with extra cream and sugar – and wolf it down while you're stuck on the highway. Guess what? You just spent $7.00 on breakfast that you could have made at your house for a fraction of the price, and you probably could have made yourself a better breakfast than the slop Dunkin' Donuts served you. If you commute into work every day and make the same stop at Dunkin' Donuts every morning, that adds up to over $1,500 in annual costs for breakfast. That money could be back in your pocket if you weren't on the road.

All told, you may be spending several thousand dollars more than you should, simply by commuting to work every day. Some companies offer commuter discounts, where the train or subway passes get partially subsidized, but even with those programs in place, you still spend much more than if you woke up and fired up your laptop in the next room. President George W Bush was asked after his second term in office what his favorite part of the job was. He replied: "my thirty-one second commute."

So commuting costs you hard dollars, not just time. Companies should be paying *you to come into the office!*

INTRODUCTION

STUFFY OFFICE CULTURE KILLS YOUR PRODUCTIVITY AND YOUR CREATIVITY

As an office worker, you have just spent the last sixty minutes commuting to work. When you finally get to work, you have to actually deal with being in the office. You have to be dressed appropriately. You have to be showered, and you must wear business casual clothing (most of the time – sometimes it's even worse and you have to wear business attire). You have to behave appropriately – no foul language, for example. You have to be politically correct and not ruffle anyone's feathers or offend anyone. In short, you have to be half a person.

Half of your identity is lost to the office culture. You really can't say what you think. You certainly can't dress or act or eat or work the way you'd like.

Let's take what I will call "ways of working" as an example. "Ways of working" is simply a strategy for how you attack your work throughout the day. Perhaps I really like to work first thing in the morning for a few hours, then I take a longer lunch break and go to the gym and make my own lunch, and then I answer emails and attend (mostly meaningless) meetings in the afternoon. I can work this schedule at home without issue. In fact, many days this is almost the exact breakdown of my workday.

At the office? This is an impossible schedule. If people see you in the office in the morning, they want to chat about their weekend, or the previous night, or their kids' soccer games. They call this "water cooler conversations" but it may as well be Chinese water torture. In the office setting, you certainly don't have a few quiet hours in the morning to focus on work, unless you get to the office 3 hours before everyone else shows up. But you have to sleep sometime.

According to behavioral economist and best-selling author Dan Aierly, you are most productive 2-5 hours after you wake up. Your brain is firing at maximum capacity. Do you want spend the most productive hours of your day commuting into work and then listening to horrific stories about kids' soccer games?

In the office you are lucky to get twenty minutes for lunch, which you'll most likely have to eat at your desk, and it'll be leftovers heated up in the disgusting work microwave or an unhealthy option from the cafeteria. You'll get pulled into meetings all day long, since you're in the office and it "might be good to attend." (Side note: anytime someone says it "might be good to attend" a meeting, decline. Find any other reason to spend your time other than attending that meeting. You are guaranteed to waste your time. More on managing your schedule in Part 4.)

I wrote this book to tell you why I believe working from home (or remotely – doesn't have to be "at home") is a much more effective way of working. I want to share with people how much better working remotely is compared to the 20th century office workday. There are so many advantages to working remotely, and from what I can tell from nine years working primarily from home, there are no clear disadvantages.

You just have to be effective. That's it. Pretty simple. If you're effective working remotely, and you consistently perform well, you can work at home for as long as you want. You can even start your own company out of your house if you want (that's a topic for another book).

But if you're effective, you will forever save those 5-15+ hours of weekly commute time. You may actually be able to read a book, or get some sleep!

What follows in this book are my routines and the methods I practice to be effective working at home. I've honed these skills – and I do believe they are skills – over a period of nine years working remotely.

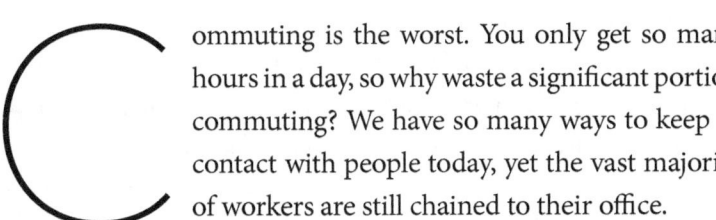

INTRODUCTION

COMMUTER PAIN

Commuting is the worst. You only get so many hours in a day, so why waste a significant portion commuting? We have so many ways to keep in contact with people today, yet the vast majority of workers are still chained to their office.

Depending on where you live in the country, you may or may not have access to public transportation. If you are lucky enough to live in Manhattan – where my wife & I lived for a year – you may be able to take the subway to work. You might be able to hop on the commuter trains of the Metro North or the Amtrak trains or the Long Island Railroad.

At least in a commuter train, you may be able to get some

work done. You can check email if the wireless signal is strong enough (or if you have a hotspot on your phone and the cell signal is strong enough). You could open your laptop and start some mundane busy work. You could read some material for work. Better yet, you could read something outside of work that you want to read.

Even using public transportation, you do not have full control over your environment. There may be loud, obnoxious people nearby. There may be disruptive people on the train or the subway. You may have to change subway lines, or you may have to stand in tight quarters if the subway train is crowded. It's certainly not an ideal work environment.

If you do not have access to public transportation and you have to drive into work, then your commute is a complete waste of time. Until Google and/or other companies make driverless cars mainstream and you don't have to focus on the road, driving back and forth to the office will continue to be the epitome of the rat race.

You struggle to get to the passing lane just to find out the passing lane is now stop-and-go. The guy that has been tailgating you for the last twenty miles has now put on his high beams. The woman beside you who was doing her makeup is now checking her text messages and veering into your lane. Commuting can be a health hazard!

Working from home eliminates the daily commute. You get

time back, you don't have to deal with a disruptive office culture, and you can avoid the pain of commuting.

This book will tell you how you can start taking advantage of the work-at-home lifestyle. You can get some of your day back. You can read that book you've had on the shelf for the last three years. You can write the memoir you've had cooking in your cranium. You can get another hour of sleep. You can spend more time with your children. The possibilities are endless.

INTRODUCTION

ORGANIZING THIS BOOK

I BREAK THE BOOK UP INTO THE FOLLOWING PARTS AND SECTIONS:

- *PART 1:* How I evolved from corporate drone to (an admittedly self-proclaimed) work-at-home superstar

- *PART 2:* Types of work you can do from home

- *PROJECT WORK:* how to run a project and how you can develop a skill set to carve out tasks to do at home. The goal is to avoid the office and the commute as much as possible.

- *SALES WORK*

- *OTHER JOBS:* you can do from home

- *PART 3:* Best practices for working effectively from home

- *DAILY ACTIVITIES REPLACING YOUR MORNING COMMUTE:* once you start working from home, you have more control over your day. In this section, I will discuss how I optimize the work-at-home environment.

- *SETTING BOUNDARIES:* if you're not careful, working from home can turn into a 24/7/365 job. Nobody wants that, no matter how much of a workaholic you are. And yes I am thinking specifically of certain co-workers. You know who you are.

- *DON'T ALWAYS WORK FROM HOME*

- *PART 4:* Non-Obvious benefits of working at home. Once you work at home for a while, you will realize the many small but wonderful benefits of working in our own environment.

- *PART 5:* What works for me throughout the day – my tips, tricks and traps.

- *CONCLUSION:* wrap it up with a call to action.

- *BIBLIOGRAPHY:* Finally, I've cited several books, blogs, articles and other material that I've found helpful over the years for coming up with some of these ideas. If you'd like to dig deeper, please take a look at some of these fantastic sources.

If you have questions on any of the material or would like to discuss in more detail, please do so by emailing me at **joemarkley33@gmail.com** or following me on twitter **@markleyjr.**

PART 1

MY REMOTE WORK STORY: HOW I EVOLVED FROM A CORPORATE DRONE TO A WORK-AT-HOME SUPERSTAR

KRAMER: "You know I almost wound up going to that game."

JERRY: "Yeah you almost went to the game. You haven't left the building in ten years."

KRAMER: "Yeah."

- THE SEINFELD CHRONICLES (PILOT EPISODE)

was once a full-time office goer, and lived the commuter
lifestyle for the first 5-6 years of my professional life after
graduating in 2000 from University of Connecticut with an
accounting degree.

Between 1998 and late 2000, I was going to school full-time
and working full-time at an Internet startup: validea.com. The
name "validea" was the combination of two words: valid and
idea. The premise of the company was twofold:

- ***TO PROVIDE TIMELY AND ACCURATE STOCK PICKS FROM THE
  PUNDITS IN VARIOUS MEDIA: TV, PRINT, AND INTERNET ARTI-
  CLES.*** For example, the stock picking website thestreet.com had
  several famous investors, including co-founder Jim Cramer, con-
  tributing stock picks on a regular basis. Our job at validea.com
  was to capture those stock picks and rate the stock pickers based
  on their public stock selections and the performance of those
  stocks over time. So if Jim Cramer picked AOL in December
  1999, how did that stock perform over a 3-month, 6-month and
  1-year time frame? We would aggregate those performances and
  determine a "star rating" (between 1 and 5, 5 being the best) for
  those stock pundits. The premise was if you followed the advice
  of the good stock pickers, you would be ahead of the game.

- **TO SHOW HOW VARIOUS "GURUS" WOULD INVEST THEIR MONEY BASED ON THE GURUS' METHODOLOGIES.** For example, Fidelity Magellan fund manager Peter Lynch, who popularized the "growth-at-a-reasonable price" (GARP) method, would only invest in company stocks which sported a price-to-earnings ratio (P/E) that was less than 2 times greater than the company's earnings growth rate. So if a company's stock had a P/E of 20, the earnings growth rate of that company had to be better than 10%. So the price-to-earnings-to-growth, or PEG rate, had to be less than 2.

Capturing the stock picks was a manual effort and required interns (like me) to read articles and track stock picks and pans. Those picks and pans were entered into a database, which was used to keep track of the pundits' performances. I was going to school at UConn at the time, and I was commuting first to West Hartford (in the founder's basement) and then to Bloomfield, CT where the validea.com office was set up during my senior year. The commute time was anywhere between 30 minutes to over an hour, depending on what time of day I traveled to the office.

After graduating in May 2000, I went to work full-time at validea.com. I had a salary that was higher than what I would have made as a first-year staff accountant and 10,000 shares of equity in the company. And this was the dot-com craze! I was going to retire in five years. I moved to Manchester, CT, closer to Bloomfield and about a thirty-minute commute. And I waited for the value of the options to grow into my nest egg.

Fast forward to December 2000. Not seven full months after

I accepted the job, the NASDAQ was down 38% in that time frame, wiping out many ne'er-do-well tech companies with sky-high valuations and no revenue, let alone profits. Validea.com was also feeling the effects of public market morass, and the management team laid off most of the employees, including me. I found out that 10,000 shares times $0.00 is $0.00.

After a few months playing poker to win rent money, I finally got a job in June 2001. I started working at Putnam Investments as a financial analyst. I moved to Brighton, MA (just outside of Boston) and for three and a half years, I took the "T" (Boston's subway) to work every day from Brighton to downtown Boston in the Financial District. Putnam Investments was one of the biggest mutual fund companies in the US. The Brighton-to-Boston one-way commute was anywhere between 45 minutes to 90 minutes, depending on traffic.

["TRAFFIC?" YOU ASK. YES, TRAFFIC. I WAS LUCKY ENOUGH TO TAKE THE GREEN LINE, WHICH IS AN ABOVE-THE-GROUND SUBWAY - AN OXYMORON I REALIZE. MORE OF A "WAY" THAN A "SUBWAY." SO EVEN THOUGH WE WERE US-ING PUBLIC TRANSPORTATION, WE WERE STILL SUBJECT-ED TO THE TRAFFIC GETTING INTO THE CITY. IT WAS PER-HAPS THE MOST TORTUROUS WAY TO GET TO AND FROM WORK. SOME DAYS IT MAY HAVE BEEN FASTER TO WALK.]

Commuting to Putnam was routinely unbearable. I started out walking about five minutes from our apartment to the T stop, and then typically waited five minutes or so for the T, and then rode the T for 35-65 minutes (depending on traffic) into the

Park Street T station in Boston, and finally walked another fifteen minutes or so to our location in Post Office Square. Total commute time could easily top 90 minutes.

During the summer, the air conditioning on the T worked about half of the time. I had to wear a suit Monday through Thursday (and I only owned three suits so this was tricky), so when the air conditioning wasn't working, I would show up to the office sweating profusely. I usually cooled down sometime after lunch.

After three fun-filled years living in Boston (and living in Boston was great for a kid just out of school – I recommend it for any newly-minted college graduate) and three masochistic years commuting on Boston's T, I decided to go back to school and get my MBA. I moved back to my home state of Connecticut and commuted from my hometown Killingly to Storrs, University of Connecticut's main campus, which is about a 35-minute one-way commute.

After finishing my MBA in Finance and Management Consulting, I took a job as a business consultant at a regional accounting firm in West Hartford, CT called Blum Shapiro. Blum has a great local reputation and this was a really important step in my professional development. But Blum was about a 75-minute one-way commute from where I was living. Not fun. The one silver lining is I got to listen to "Mike & the Maddog" daily. If not for Francesa and Russo, I may have quit the Blum job and become a short-order cook at the local diner.

So after two great years at Blum, coinciding with two horrible years commuting to and from West Hartford, I decided to leave Blum and go to work for Axon (now HCL Axon), which is an Enterprise Performance Management (EPM) consultancy. Axon at the time was based in Jersey City, NJ and employed its staff throughout the US and UK.

What this meant to me most importantly was that I got to work from home! I was officially sprung from the daily office commute.

Consulting work demands that you are on site at the client for a significant portion of the project. At Blum, I would be at the client site Monday through Thursday – commuting back and forth from home to the client site daily in some cases – and then in the office on Friday. When I got the job at Axon, I still had to show up at the client site Monday through Thursday, but on Fridays I was able to work from home.

And during slow times when we didn't have a project to work on, I was "on the bench", and I was able to work from home the entire week. I felt like Andy Dufresne after crawling through the sewer to escape Shawshank. OK maybe that's a bit of an exaggeration. But it felt great to work from home, to be in charge of my day and to get things done on a timeframe that was a good fit for me.

Starting in June 2008 at Axon, I was able to work at a combination of the client site – we were doing a big project at Barnes

Group in Bristol, CT at the time – and home. For the first time, I had a home office with all of the equipment needed to work remotely. I bought a sturdy desk, a filing cabinet, a folding chair (I've never liked office chairs), and a three-in-one copy/print/ fax machine, which I placed on top of the filing cabinet. In all it cost me about $300 to set up my home office. You can get more elaborate with your home office setup, but in order to get started it doesn't require much money. Since that time, I've been working primarily from the home office, and it's been a time-saving, productivity-enhancing joy ride. If things go well, I will continue to keep the home office my primary workspace.

Here is a brief summary of my life as a remote worker:

....

AXON (HCL/AXON)

From 2008 through 2009, I was an OutlookSoft/BPC Senior Consultant at Axon (which became HCL-Axon after HCL bought the company in early 2009). [OutlookSoft was the product I learned how to implement. It was an Excel-and-web based product, where companies could do things like budgeting, forecasting, analysis and report their consolidated financial results. In 2007, SAP, one of the biggest software companies in the world, purchased OutlookSoft for $750 million, and renamed it BPC, which stands for Business Planning and Consolidations. Nobody liked the new name.] Axon was headquartered in London, and its US headquarters was in Jersey City,

NJ. I never went into the office for any reason. I was either at the client site or working from home. I was consistently atop the utilization board and became responsible for the biggest account we had – Merck.

Merck is a massive pharmaceutical company (a Fortune 100 member), our largest customer, and a very challenging project. We had a daunting set of tasks and a condensed timeline to deliver them. We were able to successfully finish the project, on time and within budget.

Merck wanted to do even more with BPC, and my three co-workers John, Jeremy, Sankar and I saw our chance to break away from Axon and become independent contractors. We used our leverage at Merck to make Axon agree to independent contracts with the four of us. We were now officially contractors, and no longer under the Axon corporate umbrella.

INDEPENDENT CONTRACTOR

From January through June 2010, I was an Independent consultant working exclusively at Merck. This was my favorite job because I am my favorite boss. We were lucky enough to negotiate a really good rate for the six-month contract. I followed that up with another nice contract later in the year at Fitch Ratings in New York City. I was able to remain independent for about a year and half altogether.

Independent Consulting is the ultimate in personal empowerment – I had nobody to answer to except myself. In many ways, I found I was working harder when I worked for myself. It was a great experience and if anyone has the chance to work independently, especially if you have a good long-term contract in place, go ahead and do it.

And of course I didn't have to commute to an office. As a matter of fact, I rented out a condo in Miami the winter of 2010 and worked from there. My client was in NYC and I flew into LaGuardia on Monday morning, flew "home" to Miami (my permanent residence was in CT) on Thursday nights. All expenses paid. Independent consulting is a good gig.

After the Fitch Ratings contract ended, I decided I needed more training in the general consulting skills. I was an expert in BPC but needed to refine my approach to project management, leadership and develop other soft skills.

I spent a few months interviewing, and I remember even taking a phone interview while I was walking up South Beach with my feet in the water. The recruiter on the other end of the line was trying to sell me on four weeks of vacation time, and I was trying to explain to her that I had three months off that previous summer and I was currently wading in the Atlantic Ocean. Needless to say she backed off vacation time as a selling point after that exchange.

Ultimately I joined Ernst & Young (now called EY) in April 2011.

....

EY (FORMERLY ERNST & YOUNG)

From April 2011 through February 2013, I was a Manager at EY Advisory Services in their EPM practice. At this time, I was based in Boston and working out of the Boston office, but only actually went into the office about once a month or so. The rest of the time I was either at a client site or working from home. I received high marks in both utilization and overall performance rating while employed there, and I even got a chance to present a few times to the overall Boston office – once detailing the success of a BPC project and another time to talk about volunteering opportunities we were doing at EY. I'll touch more on volunteering later on.

John and Jeremy, two of my former Axon and independent contract co-workers, had joined a cloud-based EPM product company, a startup called Tidemark while I was working at EY. They eventually recruited me to work at Tidemark, too and I joined the company in February 2013.

....

TIDEMARK

Tidemark is based in Redwood City, CA, and as a CT resident, it's not exactly an easy commute. I did have to make a few trips out to the Redwood City (RWC) office at the start of my tenure for product training and to meet the team. And I have since made several trips out to RWC.

We also have an office in Norwalk, CT, which is about an hour and forty-minute drive for me from home, and that's without traffic. I've also made several trips to Norwalk over the years. But I've spent the vast majority of my time in my house.

From February 2013 through August 2014, I was a Project Lead at Tidemark in the Customer Success department. I led two significant projects for early-stage Tidemark customers, and both ended up being successful, reference-able customers: Hubspot and Brown University. I was doing the same type of project work I did previously at EY, Axon and independently, but I was working with a new product.

....

HUBSPOT

Hubspot, a marketing software company based out of Cambridge, MA, was an early Tidemark development partner. I led an implementation there for a people planning and monthly financial forecasting application. I was on site at Hubspot once every three or four weeks, and the rest of the time I was working from home.

Hubspot was (and still is) growing like a weed and didn't have any office dedicated space for consultants, and everyone on the

Finance team was running in a bunch of different directions trying to get organized. It was an intoxicating environment (in a good way), with high energy, young people and a real "buzz" in the office. But I wasn't required to be there very often, so I was glad to do my work from home.

It turns out the Finance team was busy for a reason – Hubspot was about to "go public." After seven years of existence, the Hubspot board of directors finally decided that the company had enough positive momentum to list its stock on the New York Stock Exchange. It was an exhilarating time for the Hubspot employees and I couldn't help get caught up in the mania. I felt truly proud to be a small part of Hubspot's tremendous success.

BROWN

Brown was a different story. The Brown University campus has its own intoxicating environment, but it is because of its rich history and its prestige. Walking up and down the streets of campus, you couldn't help but feel a little bit smarter. The students were all anxious and focused and positive. The coffee shops and lunch spots were constantly crammed with college students, all oozing intelligence and determination.

The woman in charge of the project at Brown asked that I be on site more regularly, and so I was on campus Monday through Thursday and worked from home on Fridays. Brown was looking to do their annual budget in Tidemark, and the project was challenging. It was my first higher education customer, so it took some time for me to understand the process, the nomenclature, and the goals. Brown was also a demanding customer – and rightly so, they're Ivy League. They pushed me to work even harder than usual to ensure the project was a success.

....

CORPORATE HQ AND SHOWING YOUR FACE

During my time as project lead, I took trips out to our Redwood City, CA office once per month at the onset of the job and slowly dialed down my internal travel as I settled into project work and became more familiar with the product. I ended up working almost exclusively from home or the client site.

Occasionally I would still head out to RWC if there was a new product launch and we wanted to have the team out to get training, or if I was helping with other company initiatives where it was beneficial to be face-to-face with product development, engineering, and other teams based in the RWC office. Plus it was nice to go out to California, especially during the winter in New England.

I feel it's important to show your face at the office. I'm going to talk much more about this later on, but I wanted to introduce the concept now. If you're a remote worker, that doesn't mean you can always be remote. It doesn't mean you can crank out deliverables in your basement while the rest of the world passes you by, and it certainly doesn't mean that you can trust your work will speak for itself. I've never heard a report or a computer program or a PowerPoint presentation actually speak for me.

Maybe someday soon your deliverables will speak, and when that day comes you really can stay locked up in the basement, making daytime phone calls to sports talk radio and enjoying the stench of your junk food and body odor. In the meantime, you need to remember that this is still a world made up of people. And people need to function in society. So you can't work from home all the time.

You'll find that showing your face in the office will have many benefits, the least of which is that you'll be less likely to get fired if the boss (and your boss's boss, and the CEO, etc.) knows you, knows who you are and can relate to you in some personal way.

You may do good work and always complete your tasks on time, but would anyone in the office know if you were gone? Would anyone in the office want to have a beer with you? Would you be up for a promotion, or would you qualify for a department transfer based on the relationships you've developed at work?

Like it or not, you must make time to go to the office, and you must develop good working relationships with your co-workers. It could end up not helping you at all – but most likely it will help you. And it may also help them. You never know when a former co-worker may need a reference letter or a recommendation or just wants to have a cup of coffee or a beer. You may be able to help him change jobs or start a new career.

....

SALES ENGINEER (SE) IN PRE-SALES

Speaking of changing jobs, I was able to do so at Tidemark. After about eighteen months in Customer Success, I really wanted to explore other areas of the company. I talked to my boss and other co-workers, and decided I wanted to work in either sales, or product, or training.

Thankfully I had been practicing the art of showing my face in the office, and I had the option to join any of the three areas. Ultimately I chose sales, and specifically the role of Sales Engineer. In August 2014 I switched roles in Tidemark and became a Sales Engineer (also called a Solution Engineer in the software industry).

This was my first sales role as a working professional. My only previous sales experience was pinch-hitting as a car salesman at my Dad's Chevrolet dealership during my high school and college years and selling gym memberships at Super Fitness in Watertown, MA just after graduating from UConn.
 In the case of car sales, my Dad (who was a Chevy dealer for 34 years before selling the dealership in 2006) always recommended that I stay away from the car business. "Too much pressure," he warned constantly. I saw the pressure first-hand, from the

beaten-down looks on salespeople's faces after a bad month and no commissions, to the beaten-down looks on my Dad's face when the economy was in recession or when the quality of Chevrolet's product line took a dip in the 1990's. He was right – it was no business for me. And it temporarily turned me off to sales in general for quite some time.

After graduating from UConn, I learned quickly that entry-level salaries didn't go very far. I was working as a financial analyst at Putnam Investments and my annual salary was a whopping $38,000. With a $750 per month rent and the usual expenses associated with a bachelor in his twenties – beer – the Putnam salary just wasn't enough. One of the guys working at the local gym was a buddy of mine from home, and he got me a job selling gym memberships and working as a personal trainer.

Selling gym memberships was much easier than selling cars, and I really enjoyed the work. Aside from a four-year stretch from 2004-2008, I have been an active person and always enjoyed going to the gym and lifting weights. (The four-year stretch from 2004-2008 is the subject for another book – the working title would be something like "My Quarter-Life Crisis").

So I knew that I could sell a car and could sell a gym membership. Selling software though? That's a whole different ballgame. I had to really know my stuff, both technically (the product) and from a business perspective. And I had to be a master presenter. And the stakes are much higher: many times you're convincing CEO's, CFO's and other senior-level executives to buy your product.

Luckily I already am a master presenter. There are few things in this world that I feel everyone avoids. Public speaking is one of those. For me, though, ever since I was a kid I enjoyed speaking in public and giving presentations. I won two state civic oration contests when I was in middle school. I used to volunteer to do the readings in church for school mass (I went to St. James Catholic School as a kid).

I honed my presenting skills over the years, took a class in college on public speaking, and I've presented to audiences of 500+ several times. I really enjoy it – and I do get nervous, but it's a nervous energy that fires me up and gets me ready to go! I like to mix in humor, especially self-deprecating jokes at the beginning of a talk – it sets a tone that I'm not too full of myself.

In my professional life, whether for big software implementation projects or for corporate events, I gravitated towards speaking in front of crowds. So even though I hadn't sold software before, I knew that I could present in front of anyone. Every project calls for several mini-presentations, too, and I would routinely handle delivering those mini-presentations.

I also had to have strong technical expertise – which I did as a project lead for the Customer Success team. I knew the Tidemark product inside and out.

Additionally, to be a good Sales Engineer I needed to be an expert in the "domain" of planning, budgeting, forecasting, reporting and analysis, or Enterprise Performance Management.

Bingo! I have that too – as an EPM consultant for 8+ years I'd helped several large enterprises with their EPM needs.

Finally, I had to be comfortable speaking to corporate executives. I must admit that this is still the scariest aspect of my job. Who am I to tell the CFO of some Fortune 500 company what to do? What I have found out though after doing this job for a while and getting in front of several corporate executives is that if you present with confidence, they will listen to what you have to say. They will challenge you, and you have to be ready for that. But as long as you have done your homework and you know your product, and you understand their business and their objectives, you can shine.

Doing your homework is a key component of any successful presentation or sales meeting. If you're meeting with a publicly traded company, you should look up their company's ticker symbol on Yahoo! Finance or another financial website. Listen to their latest conference call – the people on the call may be the people you meet! Understand their business and what drives it. Are they a people-oriented business like Finance or Insurance? Are they a gadget-based company like a manufacturer, distributor, or retailer? What are the biggest costs they have? How do they sell? By finding out answers to these questions, you will be ready to face the corporate executives.

My main responsibility as a Sales Engineer is to demonstrate, or "demo" the Tidemark product. For this area of my job, it is much more effective if we present in person. We can do web meetings to show high-level demos, but to really capture the audience, see their reaction and respond to a wrinkled brow or a confused look, the only way is to be in the same room. So the Sales Engineer job is not one where you can be 100% remote.

The meetings take up only about 10% of your time, though. The rest of the time you can work from home. 90% at home? I'll take that percentage.

As a Sales Engineer I was responsible for all technical aspects of the sale. I partnered with a sales rep, and the rep owned the account overall. I conducted technical discovery (asking questions) sessions. The discovery sessions were typically phone calls with a web meeting to show a high-level demo. 99% of initial discovery sessions are done remotely. We don't want to waste the customer's time, and they don't want to waste ours either.

So we'd have an initial call to see if we wanted to continue dancing with one another. What are their pain points? Can our product help to address some of that pain and make things easier? If we'd see a good fit, then we'd set up a deeper dive discussion, which would sometimes be over the phone and sometimes in person, depending on availability (and cost on our side).

As part of a "deep dive" discussion we may get into a more detailed demo, too. If we do that detailed demo we generally want it to be in person. After the deep dive, we may also be required by the customer to take some of their data and create a proof of concept, or a "POC". For a POC we would show the customer their data set in our product, and it gives them a better sense as to what it would be like to own the product. A POC is similar to a test drive.

The goal of a POC is to "prove" out the use case that the customer needs solved. (A "use case" example might be that the customer wants to plan for all employee expenses. "Use case" is a software term that roughly equates to a process or set of steps.) We want to dazzle during a POC, so it's important that we not only fulfill the requirement but we would also show something extra and cool and something only Tidemark could do.

A POC requires time to build the application in Tidemark with their data set, and all of that build time is remote work. When we present the finalized POC, we would always be in person for that meeting. Many times a successful POC would lead directly to a sale, so that became the most important meeting of the sales cycle.

Bottom line is that as a Sales Engineer with Tidemark, I worked the vast majority of the time from home (80% - 90%), except when I needed to make an office trip to collaborate with other team members, or when we'd go on site to a prospective customer. These were typically "day trips" as opposed to a Monday-Thursday client site cadence on the implementation side, so I was actually traveling less (and thus working from home more) than I ever had before.

....

WORKDAY

In May of 2016, I transitioned from Tidemark over to Workday, where I landed a job as a Senior Solution Consultant (presales) for the Workday Financials product. I am technically "attached" to the New York City office, which is in the Empire State Building and is eternally cool to visit. But I still live in CT, so my primary office is my home.

Workday calls my role a Solution Consultant (SC), but it's the same job as the Sales Engineer (SE) role I did at Tidemark. So the type of work I'm doing is similar, which means my Tidemark experience has really helped my transition over to Workday. I feel comfortable doing the type of work I'm doing and doing it from home.

Workday incidentally is a wonderful company with a terrific culture, and so far it's been a great place to work. If you have interest in joining a top-notch company, please send me a note.

Workday is a much bigger company than Tidemark: 7,000 + employees vs. 100 or so. Workday is a publicly-traded company and has a multi-billion-dollar market cap, where Tidemark at its peak had a market cap of just over $250 million. So it's a bigger fish. But the concepts of remote work are the same. And if you can learn to work from home effectively at one job, you can more easily transition over to another job, whether it's a promotion or job change.

....

WORKING FROM HOME CAREER PROGRESSION

I have jumped around quite a bit in my career so far. But even though I haven't stayed at one company and worked up the corporate ladder, as would have been typical a generation ago, my career path is still going in the right direction, both in terms of skill set(s) development, responsibility, and compensation. In many ways my career path has become the standard in the 21st Century. According to serial entrepreneur and best-selling author James Altucher, today's professional will change jobs at least fifteen times.

Importantly for me over the last eight plus years of my career, I've been able to primarily work remotely and do it effectively. And not only do I work effectively, but I live the way I want to live. I eat food that I cook. I go to my gym and do the workouts I want to do. I walk around my neighborhood. I enjoy my home, and being home during the workday makes me appreciate our home that much more.

In this book I will share some of these experiences with you so hopefully you can gain an understanding of how to work remotely and to it well. I took a trial-and-error approach so maybe you don't have to do the same. You can just pick up the good parts of what I've done and use those, and throw out all my bad ideas. If you want to work from home effectively, some of the techniques I use may be helpful. I hope they are.

For folks who want more information on how to convince your boss to let you work from home, Tim Ferriss does a great job of explaining how to do this in "Four Hour Work Week." Instead of repeating Tim's prose, I'd recommend you pick up his book and read about it. In fact, reading the entire book would be beneficial to almost anyone in the workforce today.

Part of what I will describe in this book is the project work I have done, and how I have been able to carve some of those tasks out and do that work at home. This was a gradual progression for me – at first I had to develop skills to work on a project, and then I was able to take those skills and do some (and ultimately most) of those tasks at home.

This was the path I took towards working from home, and it is certainly not the only way to do it. But my approach may be a good roadmap for you to unlock yourself from the clutches of the office setting and start doing meaningful work at home.

After you've gotten the work-at-home gig, that's where this book will help. I'm going to give you the strategies and methods to leverage the work-at-home experience to get more done, enjoy your work more, and still have time for life outside of work.

PART 2

TYPES OF WORK YOU CAN DO FROM HOME

DEAN JONES: "As far as I can tell your entire enterprise is no more than a solitary man with a messy apartment which may or may not contain a chicken."

KRAMER: "And with Darren's help, we'll get that chicken."

- SEINFELD: THE VOICE, EPISODE 158

Traditionally, the only work you could do at home was housekeeping. Today, there are endless ways to structure your job to work primarily from the home office. We have made great strides over the last twenty years to unlock our productive and effective workers from their daily commute and their office desk. There is still more to do, and the next generation of businesses will run totally differently than the industrial enterprises of the 1900's. But today there are more opportunities than ever to work from home, and to earn a really good living doing so.

In this section I will share with you two lines of work that can be done from home: project/consulting work, and sales – especially business-to-business sales. These are my areas of expertise, so I am most qualified to discuss the advantages of doing these jobs remotely.

But there are so many other possibilities. My wife works from home as a user research consultancy. A friend of ours works from home as a senior-level software engineer. Another one of my buddies and his wife are both in the pharmaceutical industry and both work from home. The rise of contingent workers (contractors) and freelancers have spawned entire new job categories that are primarily done from home.

No matter your job, your industry or your area of expertise, you can find a way to work from home and do it effectively. In the next sections, I will describe how you can work from home doing project work and sales work. But there are now endless possibilities, especially for the skilled technology worker. Lastly, we will cover some other jobs or careers you can do from your home office.

PART 2

PROJECT WORK: HOW TO DO IT RIGHT FROM HOME

P roject work is difficult, but if you learn to do it right, you not only will tackle any challenge in any organization, but you will also develop a skill set where you can do many project tasks at home. This is the ultimate goal, to carve as many tasks out of your job as possible that you can do remotely.

I'm using project work as a guide since I'm most familiar with doing project work. If you are a marketing expert or a financial analyst or a journalist or a salesperson, you can use some of the concepts I introduce and apply those concepts to your specific line of work.

Project work is universal. If you know how to work in a project environment, and you know how to successfully complete a project, you can do anything. People who work well in projects will always have jobs. So even if you're not currently doing project work, you should think of ways to start a project at your company. Then you can learn how to work in a project setting, and then you can learn how to do most of this work from home. Then you're "sitting in the catbird seat," as Red Barber would say.

In this section I will take you through a very high-level description of the type of work involved in a project and how you can be successful working in a project setting. By no means is this section an exhaustive explanation of the ins and outs of project work. Instead, it's a valuable primer for you to understand what project work is. It will give you a sense of what tasks you can perform now, what skills you need to learn, and ultimately what pieces of your work you can do from home.

3 Step process for all project work: Identify the problem first, then agree on how to solve it, then solve it

In order to do good project work, the first step is assessing the situation and determining what the problem really is. I cannot emphasize enough how important this step is. If you don't know what the problem is, you cannot solve it. Identifying a problem is not a simple task and can take some rigor and experience to get to the root cause of any issue.

The second step is agreeing what the problem is and creating a plan to solve the problem. Done right, this step will get every-one on the same page and assign tasks to owners who will be accountable for those tasks.

The third step is to work the plan, test the project work and complete the project. This is where you get to solve the problem – not before this step. You also can be creative with how you solve problems, impress your colleagues and customers and finally transition some of this work to remote work.

....

STEP 1 - IDENTIFY THE PROBLEM

The subtleties of identifying and solving a problem are outside of the scope of this book – but here is a pared-down primer.

Ask what the problem is, and continue to ask questions instead of jumping to conclusions. This is a crucial first step and is often overlooked. Especially when dealing with "seasoned pros" – whether managers, consultants or salespeople – you will notice that there is a tendency to categorize a problem into a bucket based on past experience. This is a vital error in problem solving and leads to more issues as you ultimately solve a problem that wasn't even the problem.

Instead of saying, "I know what you're dealing with, I've seen it before at X company", step 1 is really to listen and ask questions. Ask open-ended questions, too. Leading questions have the same effect as the urge to jump to conclusions. If you're a problem-solver, chances are that you are a smart person and you're eager to show people how smart you are. Resist that temptation and identify the problem first. You will look much smarter at the end when you have solved a problem the customer actually has.

Think of this step as a diagnostic. You know how your doctor asks you questions when you go in for a physical? He asks questions "one level deep," meaning he asks about your overall health and cursory questions about your general physical state. He does not say, "Oh I saw Mrs. Oliver last week and she has that same issue – here take this pill." He is running a diagnostic. A good auto mechanic does this same thing – he doesn't replace the transmission without doing a thorough analysis of the car and determining what the cause of the rattling sound is.

The outputs/outcome of Step 1 will be the following:

- *CLEARLY DEFINED SUCCESS CRITERIA:* these are the list of problems and how the team will measure how well you solved the problems. An example may be: "by the end of this project, we want to reduce manual steps in this process by 50%." The problem is the manual steps, and the goal is to reduce those steps, in a clearly-defined measure.

- *LIST OF REQUIREMENTS:* this is a list of what the customer team needs to do its job. For example, the system must be able to report in both US dollars and Euros. This is a requirement, or a "must-have," for the project.

If you do not have both of these items fully defined, you are not done with step 1. Throughout my career the #1 reason why projects fail or falter is because the List of Requirements isn't clearly defined. Either that or the requirements list is never truly finished, and requirements change on the fly throughout the project. The better you define your requirements, the better your project will go. This is true in 99.9% of projects.

Requirements should naturally flow out of success criteria and they should be clearly articulated. This means writing down the requirements, reviewing them and agreeing on them – in many cases agreeing officially via a requirements signature.

Some of the work in Step 1 can be done remotely. Remember this is Step 1, so you can't do all of this work remotely. Here's why: you haven't established any credibility with your customer yet. You need to put in some "face time," establish that you know what you're doing, and develop a working relationship with your customer team.

You don't have to be best friends with the customer, but they need to know who you are. And you need to know who they are, where they're from, what their kids' names are, etc. You need to know what area of expertise each project team member brings to the table. For example, you need to know who the "data owner" is if you're working with data.

Some Step 1 tasks you can do at home. Here is a sampling:

- *DOCUMENTATION:* you will have to produce a document for success criteria and a separate requirements document. You can do this at home. Other documents you may need to produce: "As Is" vs. "To Be" process documentation; data flow documents; project documents (charters, contact lists, etc.); design documents.

- *STATUS MEETINGS:* once you have done some face-to-face meetings, gone through the problems with the project team, you now need to establish a cadence for status meetings. The vast majority of these meetings can be done remotely.

The good news is, the better you do with step 1, the more work you can do from home in steps 2 and 3.

....

STEP 2 - AGREE ON THE PROBLEM AND PATH TO A SOLUTION, A.K.A. GET A PLAN TOGETHER

Now that you have identified the problem, you need to convey to your customer what you have found and ensure that everyone is on the same page. This is also critical because if you and your customer don't agree on what the problem is, you will never agree on the solution, either.

During this step reviewing the success criteria may be helpful. You may want to sit with the project stakeholders and go through your analysis of the problem and determine what would the customer's world look like if that problem were solved. Finding measurable criteria helps here too. If you just say, "well if you fix the glitch, life will be good" – what does that mean? How quantifiable is "good"? Using wishy-washy criteria is a great way to finish a project and have everyone unhappy with the result. Instead, pick something that is measurable and use that criteria to measure the before and after.

When you define your success criteria you also need to figure out how you're going to solve the problem. This may be called an Action Plan or a Path to Success or some other fancy name. Whatever you call it, you need a plan. This is often most easily captured in a project plan, but it may just be a checklist. To create a good plan, you need to include the following:

- *MILESTONES, OR KEY PROJECT ACHIEVEMENTS:* this is a high-level view of your project, with milestones to mark significant progress. An example may be: "finish building the expense process."

- *DELIVERABLES/TASKS WITH CLEAR TIMELINES:* a deliverable or task is a subset of a milestone. The Work Breakdown Structure (WBS) is a traditional method to document steps in your project, from the milestones down to the specific tasks. I suggest you research WBS as it spells out a great way to create your deliverables and tasks. For example: "build module A for the expense process." Here you want to consider dependencies, too. For example, you can't solve X until you get A, but you can't complete A until B and C are completed. So A is dependent on B and C.

- **OWNER FOR EACH TASK:** without an owner, and it has to be a person's name, not just "data team", you will never have accountability. Put a name next to every single task – this will make ownership clear. [You may also want to create a RACI document to more clearly define ownership of task groups or work streams. RACI = Responsible/Accountable/Consulted/Informed. You can look up RACI document examples online in any project management website or forum. It's a simple and powerful tool that nails down who's responsible for what. I highly recommend using a RACI.]

- **RISKS & ISSUES:** What happens if things go wrong? You need a good way to capture risks (potential problems that could hurt your project) and issues (real problems that could hurt your project). And you need contingency plans. So you need to know what to do if something does go wrong. This is critical and must be done early and revisited often. Otherwise, you could be whistling past the graveyard and not even know it until it's too late.

- **A PROJECT OWNER/LEAD/MANAGER:** you need someone to drive the project, ensure people are doing what they're supposed to do, and tasks get completed on time. This person should be identified at the beginning of the project, and this person must have "juice." By juice, I mean the leader must have enough power to get things done, to move the needle, and to drop the hammer when necessary.

You can create the vast majority of the plan remotely. You will need to present the final plan to the team, which you want to do in person, but other than that you can probably get away with doing the rest of this work from home. You may want to schedule a few web meetings to ensure everyone is on the same page, but rarely will you have to physically be at the customer site or in your company's office while you're constructing the plan or associated planning documents.

There are lots of software programs you can use to help you construct the plan, including Microsoft Project, which is the most popular. Other programs worth trying (especially if you're an anti-Microsoft person): Smartsheet, Clarizen, JIRA, and Primavera. We used Smartsheet for a Tidemark project at Stanford University, and it was good at capturing defect lists and assigning defects to project team members. I used Clarizen for the Brown project, and it was an effective tool. It mimics Microsoft Project's functionality, and it is cloud-based so you don't have to worry about version issues. JIRA is the gold standard tool if you're working on a software development project. Primavera I have not used personally, but folks that have used it have raved about it. It's very detailed and captures lots of information that you couldn't typically capture with Microsoft Project. Word of caution: Oracle bought Primavera, so expect the tool to go downhill, if historical Oracle acquisition targets are any guide (PeopleSoft, Taleo, JD Edwards, Hyperion, et al).

The best news regardless of which project management software you choose: you can do 90% of Step 2's work remotely.

....

STEP 3 - EXECUTE THE PLAN, TEST, AND AGREE ON COMPLETION

This step seems obvious but it's also where many projects fall down. Work the plan, and complete the tasks. As problems come up (and they will), identify the problem, agree on path forward and fix the problem. This is the same 3-step process I've identified for overall project work. You can break down any component of the project into the same 3-step process.

After completing the work, there will be testing you will have to do. Don't underestimate testing! Testing is the one and only way the customer will agree that the work is done correctly. If you speed through testing or if your testing plan isn't complete, you are leaving yourself wide open for problems down the road.

A good rule of thumb: testing is always the critical path in a project. If you get the testing right, everything else falls into place. If you screw up testing, you will never complete the project successfully. This may cost you money. If the customer doesn't like what you've done, she may not pay you!

Once you've completed your work, gone through sufficient testing, now you are ready to complete the project. Wrapping up the project is important, too. Whether it's through a "go-live" for a software implementation or another mechanism to get to an ending point, the customer needs to know the project is over.

Scheduling a wrap-up meeting is a good way to finish any project. During the wrap-up, you will revisit the success criteria you defined in Step 1. Hopefully you have successfully met the criteria – if not, you're not done yet! Assuming you have successfully met the criteria, you should present the output to the project team, and ensure that everyone agrees that the project work satisfied the requirements.

Wrapping up the project is important for two reasons. First, it establishes your credibility to finish a project. The New York Yankees didn't pay Mariano Rivera all that money over the years to come in to pitch the 9th inning and not close the game out. You need to prove that you're a closer. Maybe you're not as prolific as Mariano Rivera, but if you show that you can close a project, you will have a reference for the start of your next project, and that's a great way to progress in your career.

The second reason wrapping up a project is important is your customer has other things to do. Your customer put a project team together, took people out of their normal day-to-day jobs and assigned them to this project. Now that the project is over, those people can go back to their day jobs, and it's important for everyone to know that it's OK to get back to their non-project work. This is good for the team, as they will no doubt feel a sense of accomplishment. It's also good for the management team, because they can now assign those workers to other tasks, or potentially other projects.

The amount of Step 3 work you can do from home will depend

on the project. I have worked on projects where the customer wants me in a project room for most of the project. I have worked other places where they prefer I do not go on site unless there's an important project milestone. It will vary, but as a general rule you can expect to do 30% - 50% of the Step 3 work from home.

PART 2

PRESALES WORK: HOW TO DO IT RIGHT FROM HOME

ccording to an Oxford study, many jobs will be replaced in the next few years by robots or computer automation. Sales Engineers (or Sales Consultants, or Solution Engineers, or Solution Consultants, or Presales Engineers -- there are lots of names for this job) are one of the least likely to be replaced by computers. In fact, according to the study there's only a 0.41% chance that the job of sales engineer will be replaced by technology in the next few years. So, at least for right now, the job of sale engineer is "safe." Luckily, not only is the job of Sales Engineer safe from automation replacement, but it's also a job that can primarily be done from the home office.

Selling anything means that you are selling to people. This fact cannot be ignored, and sales will not soon be a completely faceless occupation, especially in the business-to-business world. A good ole-fashioned handshake and solid eye contact are still extremely important characteristics of any sales cycle, regardless of what you're selling.

What I have learned is you can do a vast majority of sales work remotely. You still need to show up at the customer site for important meetings, but for all the other tasks associated with the sales cycle and a salesperson's job, working remotely is not only possible but in many cases it's a better way to get things done. As we've noted, productivity wanes at the office, and it can flourish at home.

Here are some areas of a sales job that you can perform from home:

....

DISCOVERY

A discovery session is a question-and-answer session where you find out what the prospective customer (prospect) requires out of a new software solution. Many times you can run the discovery session remotely. In fact, from a cost perspective, you probably want to run these discovery sessions remotely. You don't want to commit resources to travel if there's not a burning desire for change or if your software won't solve the prospect's important challenges.

Similar to the way I described how to identify a problem in the Project Work section, discovery is a way of identifying a problem or a set of problems facing the prospective customer. The big difference between identifying a problem as a consultant and discovering a problem as a presales professional is that for the consultant, you're talking to a customer. For the presales person, you're talking to a prospective customer, meaning they haven't signed a deal yet. They don't fully trust you yet, and they aren't buying what you're selling yet.

As a result, presales discovery can be significantly more challenging than defining project requirements. The prospective customer may hold back some information, or may intentionally give you false information. Various people in the organization may not want your solution, so they won't help you identify their problems.

Think of an IT manager, who is responsible for maintaining the infrastructure for a company's existing systems. If you go into a meeting touting a new cloud-based solution that will not require IT, how do you think that IT manager is going to react? I'm effectively saying I'm going to eliminate the need for his job and his team's jobs. What's his motivation to help me define a problem? Maybe he is the problem!

It's important, then, when you're conducting a discovery session that you persist when you feel you haven't gotten to the root of the issue or heard the prospect fully describe the problem. Often times the problem is a level below what the prospect is willing to reveal, and it takes lots of follow-up questions, clarifying statements and challenges to get to the real problem.

There's an excellent book called "Mastering Technical Sales" by John Care and Aron Bohlig, which describes in great detail the discovery process and how you can and should use discovery sessions to identify as many problems as possible that will fit into your product's strengths. If you would like to know more about conducting a discovery session I highly recommend Care and Bohlig's book.

As you progress in your sales career, you can conduct more and more of these discovery sessions remotely. You may not be able to do this right away - it requires practice to understand what the customer's problems are and you need know what questions to ask about the customer's business issues to get to the root cause of the problems. But once you have the technique of discovery down, you can certainly conduct the vast majority of discovery sessions from your house. You may need to do a "deeper dive" discovery in person, but the preliminary sessions can be remote work.

As sales cycles become more sophisticated and prescriptive, the opportunity for sales engineers to conduct these discovery sessions remotely is a critical skill. You can get the majority of the information you need to figure out what's going on with the business, and you can craft your message and your themes to shape the appropriate presentations and demos appropriately. And software vendors have become more and more concerned about a metric called "cost to acquire customer" or CAC. The CAC is a pivotal metric companies use to track their sales effectiveness, and if you can conduct these discovery sessions remotely, the CAC goes down (reduced travel and related costs), which helps your overall sales efficiency and effectiveness.

DEMO PREP

For every demo, you need to prepare what you're going to show. You need to investigate the company through various channels, including the company's website, other financial websites, and potentially public record (if the prospect is a publicly-traded company). You can do all of your research from home. Another crucial part of demo prep is practice, which you can do from home, too. If you have to demo with other people, you may want to meet in person to get the flow of the demo down. But any individual preparation can certainly be done in the comfort of your own home.

RESEARCHING THE PROSPECT

For a new prospect, you will want to research the company and understand its business model. Without a strong understanding of what the company does, you will not effectively sell the prospect on your solution, because you won't be able to relate your solution to the prospect's industry, or sales model, or distribution channel. Without good understanding of what the company does, you are setting yourself up for not only a poor demo, but also you are potentially setting yourself up to look uninformed. If you research the company, odds are you won't look stupid.

To properly research a company, you can start your investigation very easily:

Start with Google: just type in a few google searches for the company name or the business that the company does. For example, if you're researching Amazon.com, you can type in "amazon" into google and you will get tons of information, including:

- **THE COMPANY WEBSITE.** In the case of Amazon, you have probably already been to the website, but for any company, poking around the website will give you some good information, specifically looking at the "About Us" or "Our Company" section, which will give you a company history, its values and vision statement, its executive team and board of directors, and links to financial statements.

- **ANOTHER KEY PIECE OF INFORMATION THAT IS EASY TO OVER-LOOK IS THE COMPANY EARNINGS CALL.** If a company is publicly-traded, it will post a recording and a transcript of its latest company earnings call on its website. Typically, the conference call is 30-45 minutes, with the first 25-30 minutes of prepared commentary and then the rest question-and-answer with the investment analysts that cover the company's stock. There is always great information packed into an earnings call. Take the time to listen to the call and/or read the transcript – many times you pick up info that you can't find anywhere else.

- *NEWS ABOUT THE COMPANY:* it's smart to at least look at the news headlines for the company, because there may be a recent merger or acquisition or divesture that you should know about. The company may have just missed its earnings estimate, or it may have introduced a new product into the marketplace. All of these things you should know about – so just peruse the headlines, and – if anything pops out – put it in your notes.

- *COMPANY WIKIPEDIA PAGE:* I often check the Wikipedia page of a prospect, particularly if it's not a publicly-traded company, just to get some of the history of the company and some background on what type of businesses the company runs. You can get good information from Wikipedia, like recent ownership changes, changes in leadership, and other notable events that may not be evident from the news feed or the company website. Often times, especially with ownership changes, the company may choose not to disclose that information directly on its website, if the issue could potentially cause problems with new or existing customers. In this case, Wikipedia is essential.

SOCIAL PRESENCE: you will typically find the company's Facebook page, its LinkedIn profile and its Twitter handle on the first page of a Google search. Take a quick look through Facebook – it can sometimes give you some insight into a company event or a little about the culture. Twitter should provide some useful links to recent news and any media coverage of the company –

mostly positive if it's being sponsored by the company's Twitter handle, but still worthwhile to check out. The best and most important social site for researching companies by far is LinkedIn. You can find great information, as well as potential connections to you or someone in your organization, which will be critical as you advance in the sales process. The old adage "it's not what you know, it's who you know" is still a relevant axiom today, and checking LinkedIn is a great way to figure out if you know anyone at the company.

Another site that I've found very helpful with privately-held companies is Crunchbase.com. Crunchbase is a site that provides information on venture-backed companies, mostly Silicon Valley startups at various stages of funding. You can typically find the company's funding history, who backs the rounds of funding, the management team, and other company details. It's like a Yahoo! Finance for startups.

Speaking of Yahoo! Finance, you should investigate publicly-traded companies using a financial website – Yahoo! Finance has been my default site for years, and although the new user interface is horrific, I still use Yahoo! Finance primarily for my public-company searches. Yahoo! Finance has tons of good information, including:

- *FINANCIAL STATEMENTS:* Yahoo! Finance will summarize the latest quarterly and annual income statement, balance sheet, and cash flow statements. Ninety percent of the time, the summary view is fine for my purposes. If something looks off, then

I can drill into the actual financial statements – either the 10Q or the 10K – and investigate further.

- **MAJOR HOLDERS:** you can see what individuals and funds own the greatest proportion of the company. This can be really important information depending on the industry and the economic environment. The site also shows who's been buying and who's been selling the stock, which may be a leading indicator. The investing axiom is that insiders sell stock for lots of reasons but buy for only one: they think the stock is going higher.

- **STATISTICS:** this will give you a quick sense as to the overall growth prospects, company health and management effectiveness via financial ratios / key performance indicators. This is by no means an exhaustive analysis of the company – it's merely a quick-and-dirty way to get the pulse of how things are going. It's especially useful if you aren't sure about the company's viability.

- **ANALYST ESTIMATES:** Yahoo! Finance will also show you the analysts' estimates for the most recent quarterly activity. You can see what the sentiment is – are the analysts bullish or bearish on the stock? Have they taken earnings and revenue estimates up or down over the last several quarters? Note to potential investors: if the analysts are leaning one way, go the other. If all the analysts hate the stock, it's probably the time to buy. Stock analysts are worse than tourists at the sports book in Vegas. Let's say you're in Las Vegas at the Bellagio, and you spot a Midwesterner walking over towards the sports book. You know he's a Midwesterner because he's wearing an oversized pair of jeans with a plaid shirt tucked in, bright white tennis shoes and a hat that depicts the landscape of a lake region. Follow this guy to the window and eavesdrop on him. Whatever game he picks – and he'll most likely take a favorite or an over – fade him, take the other side. If he chooses three games, you are 90% likely to go 2-1.

And that's it! Especially if you're in sales, you won't have much more time to research the company before meeting with them again – the cadence of meetings is always quick during this period of the sales cycle – so as long as you can get a working man's understanding of the company's business, operating model, history and structure, you'll be ahead of the game and most likely the competition.

Researching a company can be difficult work. Often times you end up "in the weeds" of the financial statements, i.e. the footnotes, trying to decipher a non-operating charge that affected earnings. You sometimes have to piece together several bits of information from multiple sites – particularly if the company has different separate & distinct operating entities, or if the company is a holding company with subsidiaries that are operating independently. It can be like solving a complicated jigsaw puzzle. The good news: you can do all of this intensive research in your pajamas. Research is unequivocally a work-at-home task.

....

CREATING / SCRIPTING YOUR DEMO

Once you have conducted a discovery session and done your research on the company, you need to figure out what you're going to show them, and it what order. Many times the prospect's buying team will have an idea what they want to see and in what order they would like to see it. The danger with that is you show them only what they're thinking about – so mostly about "current state" – and not exploring the future state, or the "art of the possible." It is best, then, to come up with a game plan as to what you want to show, and how you want to show it.

There are several ways you can approach this task, but it's critical you have an approach. Every customer is different, so you may have to tweak your method depending on varying requirements or idiosyncrasies. Generally, your approach to creating a demo should include the following:

A DEMO SCRIPT:

This could simply be a bulleted list that you put into a Power-Point deck or show on the screen in a Word document or on a whiteboard before you start showing the product. It could be a very detailed, step-by-step explanation of exactly what it is you're going to be doing, from screen to screen. You may opt to have something more creative, like a demo roadmap. For a roadmap, your document / whiteboard would look more like a process flow diagram than a script, but it would still show the customer the direction you are taking them. However you decide to convey the script, it is critical that you are clear. The less confusion you cause, the better the customer will follow along, and that means the customer will be engaged, pay attention, nod her head, and even potentially become an advocate of your product or solution. So be clear on the script.

AGENDA:

For any demo, in person or remote, you need an agenda. As a presales person specifically, it is your job to create the agenda. Not the rep. Not your manager. Certainly not your prospect – if you give up control of the agenda to someone outside your organization, you're giving them carte blanche to ask to see anything they want. You're setting yourself up for failure. By controlling the agenda, you get to show what you want, meaning you can show product differentiators, highlight your product's strengths, and deflect product weaknesses. It is critical that you control the agenda. You will definitely want to show the agenda to the sales rep – and any other internal team members involved in the demo meeting – prior to the meeting, so you can get feedback and ensure you're hitting all the right points. You may want to show the prospect the agenda ahead of time, especially if you have a good coach and you trust the coach. This can be a risky move, though. If your coach shows the agenda to the prospect team and they suggest a ton of changes, or are already prepped by your competition to trap you, you could end up hurting your chances of delivering a good demo. So be careful! But always have an agenda – and show it right at the beginning of your meeting, as the first or second slide in your slide deck.

SLIDE DECK / INTRO:

Speaking of slide decks, since you're leading the demo meeting, you are responsible for compiling the slide deck and/or intro. In full disclosure: I hate PowerPoint. I think slides are stupid. If you read "Steve Jobs" by Walter Isaacson, Jobs despised PowerPoint and refused to use it at all. I wish the rest of the world was more like Jobs, but alas, most business people have adopted PowerPoint (or similar software) as the de facto medium for communicating. It's a little sad, really. My feeling is that PowerPoint shows a genuine lack of creativity. Most of the time, the slides you show are polished and created by the marketing department. They have lots of bulleted lists and other groups of small words, all jumbled together. There's clear lack of white space, and typically the slide amination is enough to make you want to choke the presenter.

All of that said, you should create / curate a least a few slides to show. I tend to be as bare-bones as possible with slides – usually I construct a deck as follows:

SLIDE 1: COVER SLIDE

Put your company's logo, the prospect's logo – transparent logo, search for transparent logo on google so you don't look like a stiff with a horrible logo. Also you should have your name and title on the slide. The date is optional – I like to have it on the first slide so I can look back and see when the meeting was if I need that information.

SLIDE 2: SAFE HARBOR SLIDE

This is specific to any presenter that will be talking about a future release of the product you're going to show. It's a mandatory slide, and although it's boring, you must do it. Talk about it quickly and move on.

SLIDE 3: AGENDA

As discussed previously, this is a critical slide and really the only important slide you will show. Get the audience's heads nodding in agreement with the agenda, and away you go. If, at this point, the prospect team questions some of the agenda items, or order of events, you can have a quick discussion and potentially move some things around, but at least at this point – the day of the meeting – you won't be on the hook for presenting something else besides what's on the agenda. What you prepared is what you're going to show. If you're a highly-experienced presenter – a.k.a. a demo ninja, you can potentially throw in a few extra items at the end of your presentation that were not included in the agenda if time allows. This is not something you should take lightly, however, and certainly not something you should do if you're not comfortable doing so.

REMEMBER: you're in charge of the meeting. You can always say, "we didn't prepare anything for the use case you're describing, so we can discuss the details at the end of today's session and perhaps come back to you next week with a demo." Or you could say, "we really don't have that topic in scope for today's session. We'd be happy to follow up on that item." You don't want to offer up unlimited demos, so be careful here, but you also want to show that you're willing to do a little extra after the meeting to show you are invested in a potential partnership. Often times, after a demo is complete, there are a handful of outstanding items or requests from the prospect team. Ninety percent of the time, explaining those items a few days or a week later via email or screen shots or product documentation will satisfy the requests. The goal is twofold: to get the prospect comfortable, but also to not inundate yourself with extra work for no reason. It's a delicate balance, but by having a clearly-defined agenda, you can control the situation.

SLIDES 4 – N:

(You should never have more than 10). Other information about what you're going to show today. You can add a "NASCAR" slide- a slide showing what customers have already signed up and are happy with your product. It's a big logo slide that looks like the sponsors draped all over a racecar, hence the name "NASCAR" slide. You may also want to show a business process slide of exactly what you're going to walk through in the demo – a demo roadmap. You may have already created a demo roadmap as part of your script – this is the perfect time to show this.

My suggestion with the demo roadmap: even better than showing a slide with the process / roadmap is to draw the roadmap in front of the customer. You can do this remotely very easily using an iPad or a Microsoft Surface. I'm an Apple guy so my iPad is my go-to device for drawing things on a virtual whiteboard. I have used two different applications for iPad whiteboards: Paper 53 and OneNote. Both are adequate and provide the tools you need to sketch a demo roadmap. By drawing the demo roadmap, you accomplish three things:

1. You get out of PowerPoint, where nobody is paying attention anyway because you're showing canned marketing slides, and every other vendor is doing the same thing. You're unoriginal and boring in PowerPoint, and as soon as you hop over to your virtual whiteboard, you're doing something creative and original.

2. You're showing that you know what you're talking about. By drawing the demo roadmap, you're not relying on a predefined slide that shows the audience what you're going to demonstrate. You are a master of the material, and you can show them that by drawing what you're about to show.

3. You get the creative juices flowing, not just for you but for your audience. Scientific studies have proven that if you show a PowerPoint deck, you're triggering a response in the audience's brain, but only the left side of their brains. This is the analytical side, and after a while, it's hard to focus and the audience will drift off. However, by drawing something on a whiteboard, you are engaging both sides of their brain, because you're drawing something spatially, which engages their right brain. So you have more

engagement and more interest. Not only that, but you are also engaging your own right brain, and instead of rattling off another bullet point on a slide deck, you're creating a drawing from scratch, which jolts your own creativity engine. Now you're ready to show your expertise, you're ready to answer tough questions, and you're ready to shine. Draw, don't show a slide!

CONFIGURING THE DEMO

Now that you conducted a thorough discovery session and you have a good idea what you want to show and how you want to show it (demo agenda, demo script, demo roadmap), it's time to build the demo itself. Sometimes configuring your demo tenant is simple, and sometimes it's extremely complex. It depends on several factors. The most important factor is whether the customer's requirements fit your product's capabilities.

How closely does your standard demo content fit the prospect? If the answer is "close", you will only have a bit of work to do – maybe some cosmetic changes like creating a quick report or renaming some elements within the tenant. With Workday, doing superficial changes like renaming dimension members* is very easy, and for some prospects the prep is minimal.

[DIMENSION MEMBERS: IF YOU'RE WORKING WITH A SOFTWARE PRODUCT, SPECIFICALLY AN HR, FINANCE, OR PLANNING SOFTWARE TOOL BUILT FOR BUSINESSES, THERE ARE SEVERAL FOUNDATIONAL ELEMENTS, OR

BUILDING BLOCKS THAT UNDERPIN THE ENTIRE APPLICA-TION. EVERY CUSTOMER WILL HAVE A SUBSET OF THE FOL-LOWING PIECES OF INFORMATION, OR BUCKETS OF DATA - CALLED A DIMENSION - THEY WOULD LIKE TO TRACK: COMPANY/LEGAL ENTITY, COST CENTER/DEPARTMENT, LOCATION, CUSTOMER, VENDOR/SUPPLIER, LINE OF BUSI-NESS, EMPLOYEE, PROJECT, AND ACCOUNT (FROM THEIR CHART OF ACCOUNTS). EACH DIMENSION HOLDS A NUM-BER OF ELEMENTS, CALLED MEMBERS, THAT MAKE UP THE POPULATION OF THE DIMENSION. EMPLOYEES, FOR EX-AMPLE: THE NAME OF THE BUCKET OF INFORMATION IS CALLED EMPLOYEE. LET'S SAY YOU'RE A SMALL CONSULT-ING SHOP AND YOU HAVE THREE EMPLOYEES WORKING FOR YOU: BOB LEA, CHRIS BERMAN, AND LINDA COHN, AND YOUR NAME IS SCOTT VAN PELT. SO YOU HAVE FOUR MEMBERS IN YOUR EMPLOYEE DIMENSION: YOU AND THE THREE PEOPLE YOU HIRED. BOB, CHRIS, LINDA AND SCOTT ARE THE FOUR MEMBERS OF THE EMPLOYEE DIMENSION].

Make sense? You can apply this logic to any of the buckets, or building blocks, or dimensions associated with a company's structure. For Location, let's say you have an office in Boston and an office in Bristol, CT. The dimension is Location, and the two members of the Location dimension are Boston and Bristol.

Once you define the dimensions for an application, you can track all of these dimensions across different kinds of transactions – so paying an employee, you would want to attach the employee's name, or employee dimension member, to the payment so you could track how much you paid each employee.

As you layer on different pieces of dimensionality (groups of dimensions), you get more of an understanding as to what you're spending money on, or how you're making money. For example, by attaching the customer name, her location and her gender, you can glean insights as to the patterns of behavior of your customers, and you can analyze that information. You may then craft a promotion based on your best customers, the ones that produce the most revenue for you at the smallest incremental cost.

The prep may be significant if the prospect isn't that good of a fit for your product – which should be a red flag for your sales rep and the rest of the sales team. If you're trying to fit a square peg into a round hole, the prospect will probably catch on that your product is not a good fit, and you'll lose the business.

In the book *Same Side Selling: A Radical Approach to Break Through Sales Barriers* by Ian Altman, one of the key tenants Altman teaches is how to identify fit. If your prospect has lots of money, is willing to spend it, and seems like a nice group of people, that does not qualify them to be your customer! You need to ensure that your product is a good fit for the prospect – otherwise, the relationship will end badly. Fit is such an important part of the sales cycle, and you will find that the better the fit, the better the sales cycle will run, and the happier everyone will be at the end of the day. Your sales rep will be happy because she won the commission. You will be happy because you were able to show the value of your software, and the prospect team "got it," understood what you were saying and how it could help them. The prospect team will be happy because they've identified a good fit for a problem they're having in their organization, and your product can help solve it. It's a win-win. According to Altman, "Same Side Selling is first and foremost about finding the fit. Rather than looking to win as an individual or a company, the goal is to work with the prospect to create a picture that makes sense and looks right to everyone involved (emphasis is mine)."

At Workday, we take the idea of fit seriously and only focus on specific industries for our Financials product. We just recently introduced a Planning product, and we are feverishly qualifying each opportunity* to ensure it's a good fit, given the product is new. Workday measures itself on a few key performance indicators, and one is customer satisfaction. Every employee is compensated (or not!) based on the overall customer satisfaction rating of our customer base. We strive for excellence and will only pay out a bonus to employees if our overall customer satisfaction rating is 95% or above. So if we have 1,000 customers, 950 of them have to be happy with Workday, or we don't meet that measure, and we don't get our bonus. Over the past several years, Workday's customer satisfaction rating is 97% or above. A key reason for this is that during the sales cycle – and later during the project implementation – the Workday organization cares about fit. If you sell your product to a bunch of companies where it isn't a fit, there's no way you can get a 95% customer satisfaction rating.

[* "QUALIFYING AN OPPORTUNITY" MEANS THAT YOU ASK THE PROSPECT A SERIES OF QUESTIONS TO DETERMINE WHAT THEIR REQUIREMENTS ARE, AND THEN YOU FIGURE

OUT IF THOSE REQUIREMENTS FIT WITH YOUR SOLUTION. YOU WOULD TYPICALLY HAVE A LIST OF QUESTIONS THAT YOU CAN USE AS A GUIDE. SOMETIMES, A PROSPECT WILL BE SUCH A BAD FIT, YOU CAN TELL RIGHT AWAY. IN THIS CASE, YOU WOULD "QUALIFY OUT" THAT PROSPECT – YOU WOULD NOT CONTINUE TO SELL TO THEM. IF THE PROS-PECT IS A GOOD FIT, THEN YOU WOULD CONTINUE WITH THE NEXT STEP IN THE SALES PROCESS. QUALIFYING AN OPPORTUNITY IS CRUCIAL, AND IF DONE CORRECTLY CAN SAVE EVERYONE TONS OF TIME BY QUALIFYING OUT THE PROSPECTS THAT DON'T FIT. BECAUSE GUESS WHAT? THE PROSPECTS THAT DON'T FIT ARE THE ONES THAT AREN'T GOING TO BUY FROM YOU ANYWAY.]

And it may have cost Workday some deals (read: revenue) over the years, by not pursuing opportunities where it wasn't a good fit. But that's short-term thinking. By passing up deals where the customer isn't a good fit, Workday was able to focus on the customers that did fit, and make them happy. Long-term, this is a much better way to allocate your resources. Instead of putting out fires at customers where the product is a bad fit, you can instead nurture your already-happy customers who are a good fit. This leads to more renewals, more add-on business, and generally a satisfactory two-way relationship between vendor and customer.

So as a presales person, be careful if you're jumping through too many hoops to get your product to do what the prospect is asking. It might not be the right prospect – it may be a bad fit. If you sense this is the case, you should bring it up with the sales team and be sure that everyone is on the same page.

Demo configuration is one of the more technical aspects of the presales role. Some folks with a background in technology or software implementation may make the leap to demo configuration easily. Others, practitioners and non-technology people, may struggle. My background in software implementation both with OutlookSoft and with Tidemark helps me quite a bit when it comes to demo configuration. I've gone through enough projects where I know what will work and what won't. This is a skill set that isn't easily taught – it's a "school of hard knocks." If you're a newer presales person, or if you're not the most technical person, you may have a difficult time configuring software, and you may not be able to do this alone. In this case, you may not be able to do this work from home, and you'll have to go into the office to meet with your manager or a colleague with more experience. If you're already proficient in configuration, you can do all of this work from home.

I've built demos that sing like a bird from my home office. I find the home office to be a much better environment to get configuration work done. Many times this work requires my full attention and focus, and as we've discussed previously, you can't ever be totally focused in the office. There are always tons of distractions and you never get into a state of focused concentration. At home, you can draw the shades, turn on some soft lighting, throw on some classical music and start cranking away. You end up getting lost in the work, and before you know it, you have a work of art on your hands. As Bob Dylan wrote, "someday, life will be sweet like a rhapsody, when I paint my masterpiece." You know where Dylan wrote these lyrics? At home!

....

FIRST-LEVEL DEMOS, OR OVERVIEW DEMOS

Any first look at the product or software may require a face-to-face meeting, depending on how important the customer is to your organization. For example, if Coca Cola wants a first-level demo and is contemplating a multi-million-dollar investment, you should hop on a plane, go down to Atlanta and present to the team in person. If, however, the prospect is "lukewarm" or not considered a strategic account for your business, you may be able to get away with a remote demo. Especially if the demo is the prospect's first look at the software.

You should conduct the first-level demo after an extensive discovery session, and you should cater your first-level demo as much as possible to your audience. If you're presenting to a retailer, you should have elements of your application that relates to retail, e.g. stores or channels (direct, e-commerce). You should be able to show use cases based on your discovery that allow your prospect's team to see your software fulfil their requirements.

For example, if the customer wants to use your product for planning, budgeting and forecasting, and she wants to report on all of the planning scenarios with variance analysis, you should show her the planning process and the reports that show variances. If your product does not handle the functionality your customer wants, you should have a concise story as to how she can work around the issue, configure the product to meet the requirement, or potentially engage a third party to handle this functionality.

Workday, prior to Sept. 2016, did not have a Planning solution as part of its product. It relied on third-party planning tools like Tidemark and Anaplan to fulfill customer requirements around planning. This was a fine answer and Workday (and the planning partners) sold lots of software. The approach from a demo perspective was for Workday to show HR, show Financials, and then talk to the third party planning tools available, and potentially engage an implementation partner or an existing customer who was using the two software products.

Planning was considered a major "hole" in the Workday product. All the other big software vendors – Oracle, SAP, and IBM – had planning products as part of their suite. The fact that Workday had to engage with a third party vendor to fulfill the planning requirement wasn't the ideal scenario for them, and it certainly added to the complexity of the sale: more than one company's contract, multiple sales reps, potentially conflicting agendas. Messy.

When Workday introduced its Planning product, it was a big win for the customer, since she could do all her planning, budgeting and forecasting in the same product she is using for HR and finance: Workday. From a demo perspective, this was much better, because we could show HR, Finance and Planning, all within one product. There was no more planning hole!

The trick to all demos – first-level or otherwise – is to understand what the customer wants, know what your product can do and not do, and have a plan for the things your product cannot do. The more things your product cannot do, the less likely you will be able to get away with doing a demo remotely. It's easier to let someone down easy in person, right? This is the same concept. You don't want to say over the phone that your product can't do something if you can say that same thing in person – it softens the blow.

With strong discovery and a solid preparation, as long as your product is a good fit and there aren't many holes in your solution, you can potentially get away with doing the first-level demo from home. If the CAC (described above) is a factor and Travel & Entertainment (T&E) costs are high to physically get to a prospect's site, you may want to send the rep to the office and you do the demo from home. This accomplishes two things:

1. You cut the cost to get to the prospect in half by only sending the rep

2. The rep can be in the meeting with the prospect team to "read the room," establish face-to-face interaction, and manage the process.

Some things to keep in mind if you are going to do a demo remotely:

• Control your environment for outside noise

- Make sure you have a web meeting attached to the meeting invite and a call-in number

- Have strong wireless connection and a good phone signal and microphone

- You may want a way to communicate with the rep outside of the web meeting – enable a way to do that.

CONTROL YOUR ENVIRONMENT FOR OUTSIDE NOISE

If you have a home office setup - and you should if you plan on working from home even part time, you need to control the sound in your office during a call and/or demo. This can be extremely challenging if you have either children or pets, and this is not a step to be taken lightly. You may need to go to extreme measures to ensure a quiet place to work:

- You may have to relegate yourself to the basement. We do not have any kids or pets (yet), so I am still safe up in one of the guest rooms. But as soon as additional creatures start infiltrating your domicile, you may have to take the trip downstairs. I already have my nook in the basement picked out for when the time comes, right near the walk-out basement doors so at least there is some light coming in during the day.

- You may need to schedule a sitter or daycare or a dog watcher during times of the day you know you're going to have a meeting. Having a baby- or dog- sitter on call or available within a few hours is a step that we will most certainly have to take when we have kids and/or dogs. The unexpected will always force you to juggle kids and pets and chores and work, but if you can get an outside service or person to help you during the day, you will have less chance of little Timmy screaming bloody murder during your overview presentation.

- You may have to find a place outside of your home to field important calls or meetings, e.g. a coffee shop or another venue that allows interlopers mooching free wifi. (I realize this defeats the purpose of working from home if you aren't actually at home, but sometimes you have to adjust for the situation). In a pinch, you may have no choice but to vacate the premises and find another venue to conduct your meeting. This is a bad choice for lots of reasons, including lack of control over environment, not being comfortable with your surroundings, etc. If it's an internal call and you absolutely can't take the call at home, you can get away with this option, and I've done it many times. But I wouldn't recommend taking a customer call or demo from Starbucks.

....

MAKE SURE YOU HAVE A WEB MEETING
ATTACHED TO THE MEETING INVITE AND
A CALL-IN NUMBER

I cannot tell you how many times I've gotten on a call and there was no link to a web meeting attached to the meeting invite, or the call-in number wasn't correct, or some other completely avoidable technological issue. If you want to appear that you're a professional, especially when you're sitting in your home, you need to have your ducks in a row in terms of meeting technology. Have a phone number with the correct passcode in the meeting invite.

Ensure you have a web meeting link with the proper login credentials if you plan on using a web meeting. Log into the call and/or web meeting software well in advance of the meeting time, so you can login first and test out the connection. This is a simple matter of being prepared. Don't be that guy who's sending a web meeting link five minutes after the start of the meeting. Nobody likes that guy. He's careless and thoughtless and selfish and obviously doesn't value everyone else's time. He will not get the sale. Don't be this guy.

....

HAVE STRONG WIRELESS CONNECTION AND A GOOD PHONE SIGNAL AND MICROPHONE

I admit that I am not the best when it comes to this advice. We have Atlantic Broadband, which is a terrible internet service, combined with AT&T wireless, which is a terrible wireless service, so I have occasionally been on calls where either the cell signal or the wireless signal drops. This is very frustrating. If you have the option, ensure that your wireless signal is strong and your cell signal is solid, or get a landline for your phone calls.

In my case, my wife has the landline in her office, so I'm stuck with the cell phone if she's also working from home. However, it is no excuse. I should do a better job of preventing calls and internet connectivity from dropping. I blame myself. This is a great example of "do as I say and not as I do." It can really derail the momentum of a call if you drop off right in the middle of your big pitch, and it doesn't play well with the customer.

I recently was on a call and the call dropped – not on my end thankfully – and I continued to talk for about four minutes, speaking with great conviction about the benefits of our product. Unfortunately, the prospect never heard my impeccable delivery, and when we got reconnected, my mojo had left me and my second try at the presentation wasn't as good. These things happen in a remote work environment, and you have to be cognizant of remote work pitfalls. Avoid them as best you can, and definitely safeguard yourself as much as possible.

You may want a way to communicate with the rep outside of the web meeting

Lots of times you want a back channel to communicate with the other people on your team during a call - a way to collaborate with your internal squad without showing that communication to the customer.

The best way to do this is set it up ahead of time with your team. Define what mode of communication you want to use, and test it out ahead of time if needed. Many times texting is the best way, as long as everyone has their phones on silent and will still notice when a text is sent. Another good option is to use IM software like Slack or Jabber, but you will need to be careful about what you're sharing on your screen if you use this option.

Most web meeting software packages allow you to be very specific about what you're sharing with your audience. You can set it up to only share PowerPoint and your web browser, for example, so if one of your teammates pings you on IM to tell you something or remind you of some key point, you will see the notification and the customer will not. This type of communication is for advanced presenters and remote professionals, and I would not recommend using a behind-the-scenes communicator right off the bat. As you get better at presenting and holding meetings remotely, however, this mode of communication becomes a great way to ensure your message is resonating and your team is all on the same page.

Another good option is to get a second monitor. You can use one monitor for presenting – your slides, your web browser, your application. And you can use the other monitor as a "scratchpad": your notes, your IM communication with your other team members, and perhaps some reminders of points you want to make or key pain points the customer has. It costs money to get a second monitor, so if you are a work-at-home employee, check with your employer to see if they'll foot the bill for home office equipment. Many companies have a "desk budget" or something similar for workers, allowing them to get items like ergonomic keyboards or second monitors. It's always good to let the company pay for something instead of you! Request for Proposal (RFP) responses

Responding to a Request for Proposal, or an RFP, is another task you can do from the comfort of your home office. The RFP is every presales professional's biggest nightmare. It's a disaster. The customer compiles a list of requirements and asks the various vendors involved in the process to complete the RFP and determine what requirements your solution can meet.

The RFP is the bane of most Presales professionals' existence. It's a middling task, one from a bygone era of inefficient legacy software. Many careers have been built by "advising" companies on the "best practices" for purchasing software, and in the 1990's the RFP was the solution – a document that describes in painful detail the requirements of the company.

There are several problems with an RFP. I list two below, but there are too many to mention. It would take up an entire book.

One, many times the company describes its requirements in an unclear way. The RFP is written by a business analyst who couldn't write his way out of a wet paper bag. It's choppy. It's impossible to understand exactly what the requirement is.

Second, the RFP attempts to describe the company's requirements as the company exists today. There is no consideration as to what will happen in the future, if there's an acquisition, or divestiture, or new product, or layoffs, or international expansion. The RFP is a backward-looking document.

Responding to an RFP is a painful, unappreciated process. The rep will ask you to respond, you will spend your nights and your weekend digging into every detail imaginable in your product, and you will somehow get the response out the door in time. And the rep will give you a "thank you!" email with a smiley-face emoji. Thankfully, this painful process can be done almost exclusively from the home office. So when you curse out the sales rep for being a thankless boob, your co-workers won't hear you!

....

RECORDED DEMOS

Whether for a company webinar, internal meeting or for training purposes, you can record beautiful demos from home. Just make sure your dog and your children are quiet!

You may want to experiment with different software platforms for recording, and you may want to invest in a good headset or good speakers or a good camera if you're recording something and want it to have a polished, professional look. I've used Camtasia and QuickTime Player on a Mac, and both recording programs work well. Camtasia has a few more bells and whistles and is definitely easier to use for editing, but both programs will record nicely. QuickTime is included on the Mac, and for most recordings I use this.

I don't use a headset – I just use my iPhone headphones and microphone, which is amazingly good for most recordings. Sometimes when I'm wearing a zip-up jacket or long-sleeve shirt, the microphone rubs up against the zipper and makes a disturbing rustling sound. So when I'm recording, I remove the zipped jacket and throw on a sweater if I'm conserving heat for the day.

I have not delved too much into video recording devices and my job doesn't require that I record myself visually. However, I am considering purchasing a video camera so I have the option at home. I can see lots of value in having a video recorder in your home office. If you want to white-board something and would like to show that to a remote audience, you can turn on the camera and show what you're drawing on your home whiteboard. You may also just want to show everyone your face, especially if you've not met the audience, so they can see you and have an idea what you look like. People tend to buy from people that they have seen – no secret there.

The point of describing the several ways I do my job from home is not to give you a comprehensive list. It's to get your own brain thinking about how you can work from home, too. You may have a totally different job than I have. According to LinkedIn, there are 718,000 or so sales engineers in the entire world, with a working population of more than five billion. That's only one-hundredth of one percent, or about one in 7,000 jobs. So most likely, you and I do not have the same job.

But the principles apply. Think of a function of your job that doesn't require you to be in the office. Do that task or function from home, and report back to your boss on the results. Then continue to add more tasks to the list that you can perform equally well if not better from home. Ultimately you may not get to 100% of your time at home, but you can carve out something. Any time spent away from your office when you don't need to be there is time you save for yourself. Be creative. Think of other ways to maximize your time at home and minimize your office time, and even more importantly, your commute time. You will be happier and your work will be more fulfilling if you can focus on the work, instead of dealing with the headache of commuting to your cubical five days per week.

OTHER JOBS THAT YOU CAN DO FROM HOME

As the workforce dynamic changes in the 21st Century, more jobs are becoming "doable" from home. This is by no means an exhaustive list, but it provides you with a good understanding of the types of jobs you can do from home. I anticipate many jobs to transfer from the traditional office environment to the home office over the next few years. Your job as a smart person growing up in these changing times is to align yourself with a job that doesn't require an energy-sucking and time-robbing commute.

Here are a few ideas for jobs you can do from home. As technology improves, you may find even more jobs that you can do remotely, so keep an eye on the trends.

- *COMPUTER SCIENTIST / SOFTWARE ENGINEER:* I know several people who code from home full-time. As a non-coder, I can't speak to the specifics, but if you think of coding as a job that requires full attention and focus, it is the perfect job to do remotely instead of trapped in an office. You can make your own hours – which for most coders is a combination of late nights and late mornings. We have a friend that works as a senior manager at a very successful, multi-billion-dollar software company based in the greater Boston area. He very seldom goes into the office, and spends most of his days split between the local coffee shop and his home office. He can easily communicate with his entire team via IM and email and text message, and he can do all of his work from his laptop.

- *VIRTUAL ASSISTANT:* according to an article by Melissa Ezarik on bankrate.com, virtual assistant is a "real" job that you can do from home. As corporate jobs become less popular with millennials and freelancers and contingent workforce numbers increase, so too is the demand for someone to do admin-type services for these folks. A virtual assistant fills that need, and the assistant (or group of assistants) can do that work from home.

- *CALL CENTER REP:* gone are the days of farms of cubicles with workers fielding telephone calls all day long. If you can even get a human on the phone now when you call a customer support center, it's a miracle. Try calling AT&T. It's like the machines have already taken over. For other companies, instead of providing an expensive office space for call center reps, they will allow reps to work from home, or they will outsource the entire operation to a company like C3 Communications, which allows its workers to primarily work from home. This isn't the highest-paying job, but for someone who wants to spend more time at home and get out of the daily grind, it's a good option. It can also provide you with ample free time, so you can pursue other goals. As Bill Murray succinctly stated in Ghostbusters, "Einstein did his best stuff when he was working as a patent clerk."

- *TEACHER:* with many online courses and college programs popping up, there is an increasing demand for work-at-home teachers, too. This is a great option for accredited professionals who are tired of the daily commute and the constant struggle of classroom life. As an online teacher, you have more control over your work schedule and your environment, and you can choose what you want to work on.

- *WRITER / EDITOR:* with the transformational nature of the workforce – less folks in the office, fewer opportunities to climb the corporate ladder – many are willing to go out on their own and do freelance writing or editing. And you can do all of this work from home. Other established companies are allowing writers and editors to primarily work from home. Woodward & Bernstein probably would have been less effective working from home in the 1970's but today you can collaborate online, share Google docs or other online software, and even publish your information to multiple media, all within the comfort of your own home.

There are also many low-tech jobs you can run out of your home. If you're a hairdresser, you can set up a salon in your house. If you're an artist or graphic designer, you can easily turn that basement space or spare bedroom into a studio. If you're a plumber or electrician or general contractor, you can run your business successfully from your kitchen table. You don't have to rent that space in the plaza downtown – you can run your entire operation from your domicile.

The point is that the office or the rented space is obsolete. One day the New York office space may all be converted to greenhouses or party spaces, or may end up in disrepair. But there is no need for all the corporate drones to be in the same office space anymore, except to collect souls.

The boss collects your soul when you show up at the office, and gives it back to you when you leave. But what he doesn't tell you is that he doesn't give you back your entire soul each day – instead he keeps a small piece for himself. And day by day, week by week and year by year, you keep less and less of your soul, until you're either downsized or forced into early retirement, and by then you don't even remember what your hopes, your dreams, your aspirations or your interests are. You've lost the best years of your life commuting back and forth to a mauve-colored cubical farm. Don't let this be you. Remove the shackles of the commute and the cubical from your lexicon and start working from home. Your body, your mind, your heart, your soul, your family and friends will all thank you for it.

PART 3

"BEST" PRACTICES AND ROUTINES YOU CAN USE TO WORK FROM HOME EFFECTIVELY

GEORGE: "What, come on? You have never dated a woman that worked in your office?"

JERRY: "I've never had a job."

- SEINFELD: THE STRANDED, EPISODE 27

hate the term "best practices." It sounds aloof when you use the term, especially in front of a customer. When I was working as a consulting manager at Ernst & Young (EY), we weren't allowed to use the term "best practices" because it could get the firm sued. What if we said something was a best practice and it turned out someone came up with a better way? (This extremely risk-averse mindset and corporate bureaucracy is a primary reason I no longer work at EY.)

So at EY we called it "leading practices". It's all so subjective anyway. Who can say definitively that one way of doing something is better than another way? There is no proven way to quantify whether a practice is "best." People work differently. People learn differently.

The title of this part of the book is tongue-in-cheek. I truly believe there are no "best" practices out there that everyone can follow. There's no holy grail of how to do something. In fact, with the changing dynamics of the business world and the economic cycle and the multiple variables that make up the entire system, I believe it's impossible to have a practice that is "best" for any length of time.

Take project management as an example. In the 1940's, there wasn't a discipline called project management, and the government took on a massive, do-or-die project to create an atomic weapon. Called the Manhattan Project, it was grossly over budget and took much longer to complete than what the government officials originally estimated.

As costly and time-consuming as the Manhattan Project was, it spawned a new trade: project management. We discovered a whole new discipline, and put rules around it, gave it structure: scoping, work breakdown structures, risk & issues lists, RACI matrices, etc.

Fast-forward 50 years and project work is a critical part of large enterprises. Companies like GE and Motorola even created a system – called Six Sigma – to manage the efficiency and effectiveness of certain processes. Six Sigma consultants became a hot commodity as everyone tried to duplicate "best" practice. Six Sigma projects became the preferred way to revamp your business processes.

Twenty years later, with the advent of the Agile product development approach, companies and consultancies shifted their approach from Six Sigma projects to a more "streamlined" approach, using terms like "rapid development," "multiple iterations," and other important-sounding terms.

In twenty years, the landscape of project work will change again, most likely with the onset of another approach outside of project work (like Six Sigma for manufacturing processes or Agile for product development) that will morph into a new project management methodology. So there is no such thing as a "best" practice.

All that said, I have found some tools to ensure I'm effective and productive working from home. I have a set of routines – at this point many have become habits – that put me in the best position to do really good work.

In this section I identify three areas of my work-at-home routine that set me up for success: daily activities replacing my commute, setting boundaries, and showing your face. I would not be so bold as to call any of this "best" practice, but these methods have worked really well for me over the past several years.

PART 3

DAILY ACTIVITIES REPLACING YOUR COMMUTE

Now that we've talked about how you can transform yourself from a cubical stooge to a work-at-home rock star, and we've broken down some key types of work you can do from the comfort of your own home, now it's time to talk about some of the benefits of working from home. In Part 3, we will discuss the various things you can do in lieu of commuting back and forth to work every day. You have saved all that time – now it's time to do something with it!

Some of the activities that I cover in this section, I do on a daily basis. Others I do sporadically, and some I aspire to do but haven't found a great way to motivate myself to do them more often. Hopefully, though, this gives you a decent cross-section of the types of activities you can do now that you're not spending two to four hours of your waking day stuck behind the wheel of your car.

I organized this section into two subsections: my morning routine and other activities you can do. My morning routine is part habitual, part aspirational. If I did all of the things that I listed in my morning routine, I would be Super Man. But it's a good list and it gives you a good idea of the types of things you can do in the morning now that you're not rushing out the door to catch a train. The other activities are some other ideas that I've done sporadically or have an intent to do – ideas I've picked up from friends, reading books, and other venues.

As you go through this section, think about what you would like to do that you can't do today. Think about the time that you will save by not commuting. And then start to apply that time to activities you care about. Maybe it's simply going outside and walking around in your backyard in the morning before you start your day. Getting the grass between your toes and the sun on your face first thing in the morning sounds like a good start to me. Feel free to steal some of my ideas. Some I really enjoy, and others I do because I feel like I should. One of these days the activities that I do because I feel like I should will become "habits," or so Charles Duhigg tells me. [Duhigg is the best-selling author of several books, my favorite being "The Power of Habit", where he breaks down the behavior patterns associated with developing good habits and getting rid of bad habits. I highly recommend his work.]

PART 3

MY MORNING ROUTINE

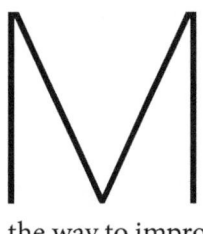y morning routine has evolved since I first started working remotely in 2008. And that's a good thing for me – it keeps me focused and thinking about the way I wish to start my day, and I can pick up tidbits along the way to improve how I feel.

If you're working from home I believe it's critical that you have a morning routine. It doesn't have to be an every-morning routine. Life happens and you can't always do what you want in the morning. You may have children, which means they drive your schedule completely. You may have to travel. You might have a doctor's appointment, or a haircut. You get the idea.

It's easy to make excuses as to why you didn't stick with your morning routine, and then eventually you have no routine, and you can't get into a groove, and you can't work effectively. Then you have to go back to an office job.

What I've found after successfully working from home for the last nine years is that you need to at least have an outline of what you want to accomplish in the morning. It doesn't have to be set in stone. I've read lots of blog posts and eBooks about morning routines, and they tend to sound (at least to me) very rigid. I don't want your morning to be rigid. I want you to "Get into the Groove" (we will discuss this in a later chapter).

I'm not perfect, and nobody claiming to have a foolproof plan for life/mornings/career/money is perfect, either. At least I admit it. But here's my morning routine, which I follow at least more than half of the time. Again, it's up to you to carve out your morning as best you can, given the circumstances of your life, family responsibilities and work schedule.

This schedule works great for me right now. Chloe & I just got married in September 2015 and this schedule is working great. So far, we don't have any kids. If we do have children (and we want to have children), I most certainly will have to modify my morning routine, and perhaps bump some things from morning to mid-afternoon or early evening.

What I've found is that if I think about what I want to do in the morning – and write it down – and then actually accomplish most of it, I feel better for the rest of the day. It sets me up mentally in a good state. After accomplishing a few (or all) of the items on my morning routine list, I feel more confident in my abilities. I feel I can take on bigger challenges. I'm ready to attack the day!

Make the bed.

I know this sounds like something your mother would say, but I read this somewhere a while back and it really does work: you may only accomplish one thing today, and it may be making your bed. But at least you got one thing done! Sometimes while working remotely, you can feel a sense of self-doubt creep in when you don't have a whole bunch of check marks on your to-do list for the day. Make sure you get one check mark right off the bat, especially if you're a checklist person.

I've shared this tip with several co-workers and have gotten positive feedback across the board. "It really does work," says one of my workaholic colleagues, who is always stressing about her never-ending to-do list. Give it a try. It takes 3 minutes, tops, and that's if you have a king sized bed and you have to make your bed perfectly.

> **NOTE:** I do not make the bed perfectly – far from it. I also realize I am not perfect, and I forgive myself every morning for it, and then I feel grateful.

So to summarize: I make the bed, which puts a check mark on my checklist. Then I congratulate myself for an accomplishment, and I forgive myself for not doing it perfectly, and then I feel grateful for the latitude I give myself and the good job I've done.

Accomplishment + forgiveness + gratitude = an invigorating start to the day. See how easy it is to start off the day on the right foot?

HYDRATE

Chloe & I went to see Jerry Seinfeld, my all-time favorite comedian, at Foxwoods when we first started dating back in 2011. As expected, he was hysterical. [I wish his show were still on. Oh wait, it's on all the time. And yes I have most episodes memorized verbatim. Thank God for TBS and Hulu Plus.]

At one point during his act I was out of my chair, doubled over in the aisle laughing so hard my stomach was convulsing and I thought it was going to burst. Luckily Chloe didn't think I was a complete lunatic for splaying in the aisle in the filled theater while hundreds of people were watching. This bit was so funny I lost control of my lung capacity. It had something to do with how older people drive however they want, with no regard for who's on the road, what's happening around them, etc. It was so perfectly worded that every sentence knocked me closer to the ground, where by the end of the bit I was laying on my back. If I laughed like that every day I would live to be 100 years old.

Another memorable bit that night was how we now as a society have to "hydrate" all the time. People are always buying bottles of water and filling up water bottles everywhere, because we have to hydrate. "Are you hydrating? I'm hydrating." His delivery was impeccable so I can't quite do it justice in print.

I bring Seinfeld's hydration bit up because, as funny as his rant was, it's actually true that drinking water is really important. Especially when you sleep, you have eight hours or so where you're not drinking any water, and your brain and body are rejuvenating, which takes energy, and consequently you get dehydrated throughout the night. You may not even feel it or realize it when you first wake up. But as the not-so-famous Japanese saying goes (I saw this on a water stand in the Toronto airport): "you don't wait until you're thirsty to start digging a well."

I have a glass or two of ice water within the first 5-10 minutes of waking up. The ice in the water makes it colder (sadly I felt the need to explain that), which wakes you up a little bit more than just drinking water out of the tap. Your body has been without water for at least eight hours (hopefully if you've slept eight hours – part five of this book covers sleep) and you need to get some water in your system.

Easy so far right? Make the bed and drink some water. Hell maybe you can do this too!

Consume either a protein shake and/or a full breakfast within 30 minutes of waking up.

For me, having something to eat within the first thirty minutes after waking up is critical. Mostly because I'm a wimp and I don't like feeling hungry, and I'm always hungry when I wake up. Not famished in the sense of true hunger, but I get a hunger pang. I am trying to read and listen a bit about Stoicism, and after gaining some Stoic knowledge maybe I can be less of a hungry tiger in the morning. But for now, I know that I'll be ready for food right away.

Eating within the first thirty minutes after waking helps me for three reasons:

1. I am always hungry when I wake up. It doesn't matter if I polish off a big bowl of ice cream the night before, when I wake up I need to eat. I've been experimenting with barbell and kettle bell strength training for the past few months, and I've noticed I am even hungrier the morning after training. Tim Ferriss interviewed Canadian strongman and strength coach Charles Poloquin on his podcast not long ago and Poloquin said he has "wild game" (like boar or yak) or some other meat first thing in the morning (Canadians must have lots of boar available). He's 50 years old and can bench press my sedan, so I'm taking his word for it. Plus, I don't want him to beat me up.

2. Because I'm currently focused on strength training, I need the protein. We're using Vega plant-based protein, the vanilla flavor that has 20 grams of protein with 2 grams of carbs and not much fake sugar. I'm also trying to limit aspartame and other fake sugars in my diet. After watching the "Hungry for Change" documentary on Netflix, I am now convinced that sugar and sugar substitutes are slowly killing most Americans. I'm not sold on Stevia being a viable solution either. Sugar and fake

sugar cannot be good for you. And honestly if I'm choosing, I'd rather have real sugar. At least I know where I stand with real sugar – we have a couple hundred years of data to show it causes obesity and diabetes. Aspartame and Stevia? Who the hell knows? In any event, especially in the morning, I try to limit synthetic chemicals in my diet as much as possible.

3. Eating within 30 minutes of waking up recommended as part of Tim Ferriss's Slow Carb Diet, which I have been following off-and-on for the past several months – with really good results. I've read other nutrition experts touting the same advice. The idea is you get your system jump-started with high-protein, low (or slow) carb food – ideally lean protein, veggies and legumes (either lentils or beans – legumes are the "slow carb" component) – and this first meal fuels me for the rest of the morning. My "go-to" meal at home lately is black beans with sautéed veggies (usually onions, tomatoes, peppers, and sometimes spinach) with 2 fried eggs on top, along with a spoonful or two of sauerkraut. It's an amazing breakfast for me and I'm full for the entire morning. Read Ferriss's "Four Hour Body" for more info on the Slow Carb diet and why protein/veggie/legume/fermented food is a great start to the day.

GET SOME MOVEMENT AND/OR EXERCISE IN.

Even if it's just a walk, I try to exercise 5-6 times per week. I don't always work out right after my morning protein shake, but I usually get a workout in prior to lunch. It will depend on what I have to get done that day. Some days I need to start cranking out work early to meet a deadline, and so on those days I'll have breakfast, finish my task (or tasks), and then go to the gym right before lunch. I'm typically in the gym for 35-50 minutes so it doesn't take much time and I get the blood pumping. Lately I've been focused on barbell work and kettlebells (thanks to Pavel Tsatsouline), but in the past I've also done some dumbbells, cardio machines (which I despise) and running outside.

If I do work out in the morning, I only have a protein shake upon waking and wait until after the workout for breakfast. Otherwise I would have a big belly full of eggs at the gym, which is not a good idea for me.

 I've experimented somewhat with doing a workout first before eating anything, and then working out after having both a protein shake and breakfast, and neither option was optimal for me. I'm too sluggish if I don't eat anything and I'm too full during my workout if I eat everything first. You may want to experiment to see what works best for you and your body.

Another option for getting moving in the morning is to do some mobility work. You can check out Kelly Starrett's website mobilitywod.com for further details – subscription required – or you can pick up his book "Becoming a Supple Leopard." Starrett is a physical therapist and heads up the world-class San Francisco Crossfit gym. I'm not a Crossfit guy, but Starrett's advice for movement and mobility is important for any adult, specifically those of us that are sitting in a chair in front of a computer all day.

The human body was not made to sit in front of a computer all day. Sitting, especially in a position with your arms forward – and thus your shoulders slumped forward – does immeasurable long-term damage to your health. If you're experiencing back pain, neck pain, shoulder pain, tight hips, ropey ankles, or any other ailment that could be caused by sitting in a chair for eight hours per day, you need to check out what Kelly is teaching. You can go onto youtube.com as well and check out some of his older videos for free.

Start the day standing up.

Most of the time I like to start standing at either our sit/stand desk or the counter instead of starting off the day seated. I feel like my energy level is higher when I start standing, and when I eventually get tired of standing up, I'll just grab a seat. I probably average 80% standing / 20% sitting during the day when I work from home. The standing percentage goes down precipitously when I'm at the office or a customer site, as most of the world has not caught on yet to the benefits of standing and the detriment of sitting throughout the day.

And I almost always take meetings on foot. I feel much more energized when I'm talking to someone on the phone and I'm standing up. "Sitting is the new smoking" as Kelly Starrett and countless others say. "Motion creates emotion" as they say in "Boiler Room." Those are a couple of good phrases telling you to get off your ass.

It's true, at least from my experience. When I'm standing up (or even pacing around a little bit – not obsessively, but maybe moving a little while talking or presenting), I feel more alert, have better energy and seem to absorb more information. I ask better questions. It's such an easy trick, too. Just get up out of your seat.

We bought a really fancy sit/stand desk on Amazon, which works great. You probably don't need to buy something quite so expensive (if I remember correctly we paid over $600), and you may be able to put together a makeshift operation at home using a counter and a couple of books. I used the kitchen counter and a big box when Chloe & I were both working from home in our tiny apartment in New York City. As long as the height of the structure is OK for you, then you don't need an "official" sit/stand desk. Actually as I think of it, our sit/stand desk is a bit obnoxious.

Avoid Facebook.

I don't log into Facebook until 5:00PM local time at the earliest. I've been good about doing this lately and it's made a big difference. Prior to implementing this rule, when I was building a custom demo for a prospective customer, I used to find the need to distract myself. Typically, the building process would take a bit longer than I'd like, or I was struggling to get something to work. I used to take those moments of inactivity and log into Facebook to see what everyone wanted me to think their life was about. And then I'd find myself spending 30 minutes (or more) on Facebook, checking out pictures of people I don't even talk to. So no more Facebook for me during the workday, especially in the morning.

Most people are at their most productive between the second and fifth hour of being awake according to Airely. I've named this window (which I've only said to myself, until now), and I call it my "Productive Mental Morning Window". You shouldn't waste that peak time on stupid stuff. And Facebook is the epitome of stupid stuff.

There's an entire section in this book on *First Thing's First,* modeled after the late Stephen Covey's old book of the same name. The book is now out of print I believe, but I still have a copy if you want to borrow it. The book was a bit too "preachy" for me – like Stephen Covey never did anything wrong. Maybe he never did do anything wrong. I don't want to speak ill of the dead. In any event, he created a quadrant for types of activities:

1. Urgent and important

2. Not urgent and important

3. Urgent and not important

4. Not urgent and not important

I go into more details about the *First Thing's First* concept in part five. Covey's idea in a nutshell is that you want to focus as much of your energy as possible on #2 activities, and avoid

#3 activities and especially #4 activities. #1 activities are unfortunately unavoidable. Covey wrote the book in 1997, so Facebook wasn't around yet. Zuckerberg was probably in middle school actually. If there ever was a # 4 activity, it's Facebook. It's certainly not urgent and it's certainly not important. If it were urgent, you would get a phone call or a text message. If it were important, it may have been a phone call, email or even a face-to-face conversation. Yes, people still have those. And in-person conversations are not #4 activities, especially in the business world.

Another benefit to avoiding Facebook during the day? I don't miss it. It's amazing how much time I would waste on Facebook, and now that I don't log in at all during the day, I feel liberated.

COFFEE, COFFEE, COFFEE, COFFEE

I'm a slave to my morning java and I'm not ashamed to admit it. Plus, I read that it's good for your metabolism and it may help to prevent the onset of Parkinson's disease if taken in large doses (which is typical for me).

And yes I'm using the Parkinson's disease prevention angle as an excuse. I definitely drink too much coffee, but I love it, and it loves me back. Maybe one day I'll wean my way off of the aromatic elixir, but no time soon.

I have also read that the antioxidants in coffee are stronger and more powerful than just about any other source of antioxidants. So instead of pouring a big glass of orange juice, packed with vitamin C but also with an unnatural amount of sugar, pour yourself a cup of Joe. Your immune system will thank you.

I drink coffee black as nature intended. I know some people need their cream and sugar in their morning cup, and I used to make coffee like that too when I was a child. I'm an adult now. I like the taste of coffee – I don't need to dumb it down with cream and added sugar. "I like my sugar with coffee and cream" is a great line but a horrible way to drink coffee. And don't get me started on artificial sweeteners. Also, when you order black coffee in a coffee shop, you can say fun things like, "straight up, just like my scotch" or "hot and black, just like my ex-girlfriend." My wife doesn't appreciate the latter.

We don't do anything fancy currently with the coffee at home. As a matter of fact, we probably break lots of rules of good at-home coffee making. We buy the ground coffee. We keep the ground coffee in the freezer. We use a cheap-o Black & Decker coffee maker. We use tap water. Coffee aficionados would cringe.

But I can make a whole pot of coffee in about two minutes. Two minutes to wait for coffee is long enough. I don't need to be grinding beans and filtering water and testing temperatures and whatever else coffee snobs do. I already feel snobby enough with my $600 sit/stand desk.

One caveat with coffee is drinking it after 3:00PM or so. The half-life of caffeine in coffee is four hours, so if you have a coffee at 3:00PM, the caffeine will still be in your bloodstream at 11:00PM. Depending on when you go to bed, this could affect your sleep. If you can avoid having that afternoon caffeine boost, you should – you will sleep better. In fact, you'd be better off napping instead. More on that in part four.

Give yourself time to check work email, personal email, and LinkedIn – if you have time available.

I do this almost every morning. I like checking my personal email (still a Yahoo! account, if you can believe that) because I subscribe to some great blogs/services that I'll read in the morning if time allows. Seth Godin, whose blog is usually short and pithy, and James Altucher are two of my favorites.

I like to check LinkedIn because I've been publishing posts there lately and want to check my traffic stats. Also there are lots of good articles and updates in the morning. This whole circuit of email/email/LinkedIn should take no more than 20 minutes. If you find yourself spacing out or taking longer than that, realize how much time you're taking, and adjust.

The great part about giving yourself time to check LinkedIn and email in the morning is that you still feel connected to the world. You may not have a call with a customer or prospect or co-worker when your workday starts. So checking in with people, whether through a quick email reply or a LinkedIn "like" or "comment" is a nice way to keep in touch with your network.

GET TO WORK!

If you have a good game plan as to what you want to attack in your day (we will talk more about this in a later chapter), you will know exactly what you need to do that morning. So start cranking! If it seems insurmountable, it probably isn't. Just break it down into small pieces, go slow, and do one thing at a time. Ideally you can turn off your work and personal email at this point (since you've already checked it), and you won't have any other distractions since you aren't on Facebook.

One peer pressure you may get is to log onto your company's messaging app, since remote workers are communicating more and more this way. Our company uses Jabber, which is a decent tool, and I've used Slack in the past, which is a great product. I will typically open the IM app right after work email, personal email and LinkedIn, but then I shut it down if I have a really complicated task to perform. I need to focus. So do you.

The human mind is physically incapable of multitasking (even though some of my co-workers and friends disagree), and getting distracted by someone pinging you on IM can set you back much more than you think. If you're "in a groove," you can get completely thrown off track by distractions, and sadly you may not get back on course. So shut down the apps, the email and the social media and get your brain firing and keep your keyboard popping!

You may think this is quite a list for a morning routine. Two things:

1. I don't do all of these tasks every morning. If I did, then I would be like Drago at the beginning of Rocky IV. I'm more like Drago at the end of Rocky IV. I'm not a machine. I'm a man.

2. Since I'm working remotely, I'm saving at least an hour of commute time. So I've been given a great gift as a remote worker: the gift of time. Between eating breakfast, getting in a workout and my email/email/LinkedIn circuit, we're talking about 90 minutes. So instead of getting in my car, dealing with traffic or wasting my productive mental morning window on the subway, I'm putting myself in good physical and mental condition to get my work done. And folks, this is a book about getting your work done effectively. You will not see the word "efficiently" in this book at all. I'm not programming you like a machine on the factory floor. I'm showing you what I do to get my work done, have a work/life balance and take advantage of the benefits of remote working.

PART 3

OTHER ACTIVITIES YOU CAN DO FROM HOME

WRITE DOWN 10 IDEAS

This is James Altucher's practice and I've been horrible about keeping up with it. This is more of an aspirational habit that would transform my thinking and turn me into an idea machine. I started off using this tactic fairly regularly after reading Altucher's book "Choose Yourself," but my idea engine has stalled. Now and again I write down some ideas, not always ten, and I always feel better after I write them down. If you can keep up with it, it's a great practice. I found that it took a little too much of my mental energy to do in the morning, and by the end of the day my ideas weren't flowing.

I haven't completely given up on this behavior yet, but in full transparency I didn't want to recommend something I'm not currently doing. This is the classic "do as I say and not as I do" advice that you've gotten from your parents, teachers, bosses and other authority figures your whole life. I don't want to be like them – no offense to your parents.

For those of you who don't know James Altucher, he is a best-selling author, speaker, investor, podcaster, and all-around genius. His most famous book is "Choose Yourself," and if you have the opportunity to read this book it may literally change your life.

Altucher rails on the traditional "conventional wisdom" of the 20th Century working class life. Buy a house, put money into your 401(k), earn a steady paycheck, and hope for the best: that's the way many people today are still living, even though it sets you up for potential catastrophic downside.

Altucher offers an alternate solution, and that is to "choose yourself". It doesn't mean quit your job today and start making & selling Native American headdresses out of your home (although that's not a terrible idea). What it does mean is planning for success. It means not being a slave to the corporation.

His practical recommendation for "choosing yourself" is to write down ten ideas per day. He warns the reader that your ideas at first will be really bad. No matter. You are not writing down ten good ideas, just ten ideas. If you follow the practice for six months, Altucher posits that you will become an "Idea Machine." And then the world will be your oyster. There's more to it than that, and I encourage you to read the book for details.

I don't write down ideas every day but I've been decent about writing down some ideas some of the time. Again, I'm human and sometimes I don't do this. I don't beat myself up over it. James recommends 10 per day, since that's what works for him. I hope to someday get to writing down 10 per day on a more consistent basis, but for now, I'm happy writing down the ideas I write down on the days I do it.

I will say that writing down 10 ideas is not always something I do in the morning. Truly I would love to grab my notebook right after breakfast and start jotting down ideas. But at least lately, I've been writing them down after dinner, usually while drinking a glass of beer or wine. Altucher doesn't drink anymore, but I do, and I feel like a glass of beer (not 4 glasses, though, 1 glass) gives me a bit of creativity and relaxes my mind just enough to come up with 10 ideas.

Now, these may not be great ideas. And maybe that's because I'm writing them down at the end of the day when my brain is tired, while drinking wine. Maybe I should be writing down my ideas in the morning. This is an area I can experiment a bit more and see what works best. I think the important point is that you try to follow the practice, and not worry so much about what time of day you perform the practice.

The concept behind writing down ten ideas per day is that you need to exercise your "idea muscle" as Altucher describes. The same way you need to exercise your body, either through walking, swimming, mobility movements or resistance training, you also need to exercise your brain.

If you stop working out, your muscles atrophy. Unfortunately, this happened to me in early 2016 when I had surgery on my right knee. I had to be off my leg – non-weight-bearing on crutches – for six weeks. As a result, my right leg muscles started getting stiff, and started to ache and feel weaker. I was doing as much as I could to move around, stretch and do some light mobility work during the six-week stretch, but I still experienced significant loss of strength and flexibility.

Extrapolate that feeling and result I got from six weeks of inactivity to the modern person's savagely sedentary lifestyle. Can you imagine how much your muscles atrophy by sitting all day?

Extrapolate further what that would mean if you weren't exercising your brain. If you're not reading, and writing, and thinking, your brain may be atrophying much the same way my right leg shriveled.

So maybe you don't have to follow Altucher's advice to the letter and write down ten ideas every single day. He touts that by writing down ten ideas per day, you can become an "idea machine" in six months. So if you only write down five ideas per day, it may take you a year to become an "idea machine."

Fear not. No matter your time frame, by becoming an idea machine you may be able to essentially chart out your career, start your own business, or figure out a way to work from home forever. Altucher calls today's landscape the "Idea Economy" and those with the best ideas will do best and be in the best position to prosper.

TAKE A COURSE

You can take a course at the local community college, or take a cooking class. These may be viable options for you, especially if you are looking at a career change or if what you're interested in requires you to work with your hands.

For other topics, like learning new technology or learning more about business, or math, or science, you can go online and find tons of interesting topics on many great educational sites. I have taken a few courses on Udemy, and the content is superb. Khan Academy, Lynda.com, Codeacademy and others are good options. Because you have some extra time doesn't mean you should increase your Netflix viewing or watch that season of Seinfeld for the twentieth time. The courses available online are typically well curated and full of relevant content. And you will learn more in one Udemy course than you will in four seasons of House of Cards, unless you're looking to learn how to cover up a murder. House of Cards would be better for that.

READ A BOOK

You can get more reading done if you're not stuck commuting. Take advantage of it and read about your industry, or read something else that interests you. I try to read for at least an hour per day, and I choose from the following media: physical books, kindle books, online articles, online newsletters, blogs, and audiobooks.

PHYSICAL BOOKS: I love the feel of a physical book. I know I'm supposed to have everything on my kindle now, but I like to turn the page, I like the smell of a book, and I like that I'm not looking at a screen for a bit. I usually choose physical books for my nighttime reading, which tends to be biographies and fiction. Nothing gets me sleepier than reading about someone's childhood. It could be Abe Lincoln, one of the most fascinating humans ever. In Doris Kearns Goodwin's "Team of Rivals" – an excellent book and truly captivating – if you read the first part of the book about his childhood and can't fall asleep, you have a serious magnesium deficiency.

I also will buy a physical book if I feel like it's too complicated to read the kindle version. If I need to study complex graphics, for example, I'll choose the physical book. When I read "The (Mis)behavior of Markets" by Benoit Mandelbrot, a brilliant mathematician, I had to buy the physical copy. Some of the concepts he introduces would be lost on a digital copy.

KINDLE BOOKS: for books that I want to read during the day or just after my workday, I will sometimes choose a Kindle book. If I know I have to travel for work – especially train and plane rides, I'll put a book on my Kindle and have a lightweight option. Typically, my Kindle choices are business- or health-related lately, and I'll sprinkle in a biography or two. I go through phases where I don't read on the Kindle for months and then I pick it up again and fly threw a few books.

ONLINE ARTICLES: I've found LinkedIn is a great source for articles relating to business, entrepreneurship, leadership, and technology. Sometimes in my LinkedIn feed I'll just peruse a few articles to see what the thought leaders are discussing. "Influencers" like Richard Branson, Arianna Huffington, Bill Gates, Tony Robbins, and Dharmesh Shah are some of my favorites for compelling content.

ONLINE NEWSLETTERS: Currently I'm a paying subscriber to one newsletter: The James Altucher Report. This is an excellent newsletter, packed with new and exciting content every month on things like entrepreneurship, creating multiple income streams, doing what you love, and learning to benefit from the overarching trends in today's marketplace. I highly recommend his newsletter – it may change your life. I also subscribe to a few free newsletters, which are sometimes good and sometimes not, and not really worth mentioning.

BLOGS: I also follow Altucher's blog, which is a daily post. His blog post is essentially a big confessional, but it's also entertaining and within his seemingly manic-depressive musings, it usually provides a lesson.

Seth Godin's blog is one I read every day. I haven't missed a post in over a year. His daily posts tend to be pithy and impactful – the perfect combination for an early morning shot of written adrenaline.

Other blogs I follow, albeit not as closely as Godin and Altucher:

- *TIM FERRISS'S "FIVE BULLET FRIDAY"*, which is more of a list than a blog, but it usually links to interesting content.

- *MARK SUSTER'S "BOTH SIDES OF THE TABLE"* – about venture capital and entrepreneurship. He tells some biting truths about Silicon Valley and pulls no punches.

- *NOAH KAGAN:* one of Ferriss's buddies and founder of App Sumo, he's always entertaining if not a bit narcissistic. He did introduce me to Myles Apparel, which makes the best shorts ever.

- *ADAM GRANT'S "GRANTED"* – if you've read any of Grant's books, his focuses are on generosity and introversion/extroversion. Very interesting and sometimes over my head.

AUDIOBOOKS: I realize this isn't technically "reading." Semantics. Nobody likes a smartass — just go with me on this. Audiobooks are a great option if you can't read while you're doing something else, but you still want to exercise the gray matter. I've listened to audiobooks while getting ready for the day, while working out, and while traveling — especially driving.

One caution with audiobooks: they can be long. Like 35 hours long. So if you choose, choose wisely.

HOUSEHOLD TASKS

In part four we will talk about controlling your diet, but one of the benefits of being home is you can cook your own food, in your own kitchen. I love to cook, and although I'm not a trained chef, the meals I make are usually tasty and healthy. Part of cooking is the prep and the cleanup, so I'm constantly chopping onions, running the dishwasher and doing the pots & pans in the sink. Controlling the overall synchronousness of the kitchen is my primary area of responsibility.

You're home. So if you need to take out the trash, mow the lawn, trim the hedges, vacuum the floor, you can do it. Some of these tasks may only take a few minutes, and you need to take breaks anyway. Instead of spacing out for a few minutes, you could accomplish a few items on the household to-do list. Your spouse will thank you, and you'll be happier because you don't have to do a huge chunk of housework at once – you can spread it out throughout the day or even the week.

Hopefully this gives you a flavor as to the types of activities you can do from home. This obviously is not an exhaustive list – it's what I typically do, and it works for me. Please steal some of my ideas if you like them, and add in your own favorites. This section is meant to stimulate your thinking to unearth some activities that you probably want to do but you can't do today because you're stuck on a train.

Now that we've discussed some activities you can do from home, let's discuss how you should communicate with your co-workers, including your boss. You need to establish a cadence, and it needs to work for you and for your colleagues. You need to set boundaries, and you need to keep them, and your co-workers need to respect them. Otherwise, the joy of working from home will quickly be eclipsed by the sorrow of being "always on."

PART 3

SET BOUNDARIES

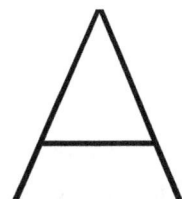

As a remote worker, I've seen many times where my colleagues will wake up at 5:30AM, check email first thing in the morning, and start working. Maybe they'll grab a quick bagel or pastry for breakfast.

Then they'll work right through lunch, pounding a protein shake and coffee drink at 2:00PM. Then they'll power right through dinner and have a granola bar at 9:30PM with a glass of wine. They'll finally power down at 11:30PM only to repeat the same process again the next day. Does this sound familiar?

If it does, I have news for you: this is not a sustainable way to live. Not eating right (or enough, or eating while working) + not putting down your laptop for 17 hours + not getting enough sleep (and you're probably not sleeping well from 11:30PM – 5:30AM anyway because you're thinking of work) is a recipe for disaster.

Sadly, this was once me. I was on a project for a very prestigious customer and the project was going south for a number of reasons. But I was in charge and I needed to ensure we got back on track. So I followed the above formula for about 9-10 months straight. I figured that was the only way to get the job done.

What was the result? I was overtired, overworked, overstressed and my brain was mush. I had burned myself out. I was a puddle. I was doing 5 things at once and doing them all badly. My mind was racing from task to task like a gerbil on meth. I was making things worse on my project and not better.

Then I got some great advice from our team leader, Scott. I mentioned to him that I always got an email at night around 9:00PM from the customer about something that was going wrong, and I would stay up all night trying to fix it, usually resulting in me making a stupid mistake at 2:00AM. He said, "Joe, just don't check your email at 9:00PM."

It was like a light bulb went off. I felt like Gru in "Despicable Me" (if you haven't seen the movie, do yourself a favor and watch – Steve Carrell absolutely kills it). I didn't have to answer a 9:00PM email at 9:30PM or 11:45PM that night. I could instead choose to set a boundary.

That's what got me started with my setting boundaries routine. Again, this is what works for me, and I admit that I almost never stick to this fully. But I'm trying. It's really difficult, but when I do stick to my plan, I perform better and I do better work. I am more effective.

So here's what I do to set boundaries while working from home:

PART 3

ESTABLISH AN INFORMAL SERVICE-LEVEL AGREEMENT (SLA) WITH YOUR CO-WORK-ERS, YOUR BOSS AND YOUR CUSTOMERS

You don't have to be as formal as documenting an official service-level agreement, but the idea is the same. When you start a customer engagement, you should let the project team know typically how long it will take for you to reply to an email or return a call. A good rule of thumb is to answer emails and respond to phone calls by the end of the working day.

This also goes for co-workers. I find lots of times that I need a window of time to concentrate, and replying to the latest fire at the latest customer from the "IMPORTANT!" email from a co-worker in distress does not help me focus.

For situations like these, I think about the sign that was posted behind the counter at "Java Joint", the coffee shop at UConn across from the School of Business. Usually students would be running late and scrambling frantically to get their caffeine fix.

[I ALSO NOTICED THAT IT WAS THE ONES RUNNING LATE WHO USUALLY HAD THE MOST COMPLICATED AND TIME-CONSUMING COFFEE ORDERS. BUT I DIGRESS.]

Amidst the mania, the same Java Joint coffee crew calmly took care of each order one by one, and got the drinks out as quickly as they could. They hardly ever got an order wrong and the wait time was very consistent. You know why? They didn't panic every time a customer panicked. They realized that panic did not have to be met with additional panic. In fact, the opposite is usually true: if you meet panic with calm, you are more likely to get a good outcome for everyone.

You know what that sign said behind the counter? "Poor planning on your part does not constitute an emergency on mine."

Brilliant! Absolutely brilliant. And you know what? It's the truth. Sometimes you have to break this rule, but the vast majority of the time, like 99% of the time, this rule holds. The panic-stricken co-worker with the huge problem that has to be solved or the world will end? You know what? The world never ends. It's always OK.

Sometimes your co-worker can deflect the issue on a customer call or during a meeting. Sometimes he can figure out a workaround prior to the meeting. And sometimes he has to eat crow. Eating crow is not a bad thing. It's a character builder. I've eaten so much crow over the years I could probably pass for Brandon Lee (minus the bullet hole in the head – and pun intended). And now I'm usually prepared for meetings, and maybe someday my co-workers will be, too.

It's important to establish these time frames (not rules – because co-workers and especially customers don't like when you dictate rules) up front and communicate them often. It's equally important to communicate well in advance if your typical "SLA" is going to be changing for any period of time. A good example is if you're going on vacation. You don't want your boss or your customer calling you on the beach? Don't forget to tell them you're going to the beach!

The following is a rough "SLA" outline of what I communicate to co-workers, customers and prospects. You may also find this helpful for communication with roommates, friends and family members, too.

My typical SLA:

For emails, although I communicate an end-of-day response deadline, most of the time I reply within 2 hours. You know what I noticed about this? Lots of times if you wait 2 hours, the person with the question will actually have solved the problem themselves. Then you get two emails: one that asks the question, and then a second that says he figured it out.

See, you're really accomplishing two things here. You're letting them write down the problem on paper (or email, whatever), which let them think about it some more, and you're making him feel good by solving his own issue. You're like Buddha.

For phone calls, I will also communicate an end-of-day response policy. The reality is that unless I'm completely engrossed in something, a.k.a. I'm "in the groove", I will answer the phone during the workday. I figure if someone puts in enough effort to actually pick up the phone, find my contact info and physically call me, it must be something worth discussing. And I admire them for actually picking up the damned phone.

Not enough people call other people anymore. If you want to get a hold of someone, try calling them. Sending a LinkedIn "in-mail" is weak and sending a text message is bush league. Pick up the phone. I respect that. Consider calling when you want to get a hold of someone instead of email. It's much easier to dismiss an email than a phone call.

I consider IM much less formal and if I'm on IM, that's my own fault for logging in, so I'll reply back right away. If I absolutely need quiet time or I have another obligation, I will log off. Very important point: if you're on the phone and doing a web meeting, especially with your CEO, and you're sharing your screen, log off of all IM services. Believe me, this is not a hypothetical. Just please take my word for it. It can be super embarrassing if someone happens to see something he shouldn't.

I try to never answer a call or email prior to 8:00AM or after 9:00PM (unless it's a family member or one of my buddies about meeting for a drink). I am strict about this to give myself 11 hours of non-work communication. That doesn't mean I'm not working late some nights. I am. I just turn off the email and don't answer the phone.

Check In, Give Credit and Take Blame

Because you are blessed to work from home, you may feel like you are as free as a bird, and that you have no real responsibilities because your boss isn't breathing down your neck. Nothing could be further from the truth. If anything, you are more scrutinized because you're working from home.

As a responsible working adult, you need to do your work, and because you're not in the office you are more likely to do it effectively. But if you do not communicate to your boss, your co-workers and your customers what work you have done, you will not get credit for your work.

Not once in my work-at-home career has a deliverable of mine gone unnoticed. I am not in the habit of bragging about my work, and quite often I will give credit to others for a great team effort. But I also know I have been given a great gift: the gift of not having to go into the office. I want to keep that gift, and the best way to maintain a work-at-home situation is to do good work and tell people you have done good work. It's that simple.

Nothing ruins productive work quicker than not telling anyone about it. I don't mean you need to brag about all your accomplishments. Quite the contrary. I agree with Jim Collins and others that you should give credit to others whenever possible.

However, it's possible to give others and you credit for tasks and/or projects, and if you're working from home, you should take the opportunity to do that. If you fail to let people know what you've done, you may find it difficult to get a raise, promotion or the next job you want. You may even get fired. I've seen many, many examples of remote workers doing a terrible job of checking in. Guess what? They no longer work with me. Be "Abe Lincoln" – check in periodically on your schedule

Colin Shaw wrote an interesting article on LinkedIn a couple of years ago titled "Secrets of Being Promoted and Earning More Money." Shaw is a CEO and author/speaker who has three personas he sees that encapsulate the vast majority of the workforce:

The Showman

The showman is the guy who doesn't do anything but takes all the credit. Showmen are everywhere in life, especially in sales. Some showmen are so good at being showmen that it takes years for others to realize that they're not doing any work – they're just talking about the good work that others have done.

Think of someone like Chris "Birdman" Anderson. He averaged 17 minutes, 5 points and 5 rebounds over his career, but because of his ridiculous appearance – peppered with tattoos and wearing a Mohawk – and his antics on the court, NBA teams kept signing him to contracts, and the fans loved him. But guess what? He stunk.

The Implementer

The implementer is the person who does all the work behind the scenes and never gets any credit. These are the classic workers in the organization. These people need people like me to stick up for them and tell others about the good work they're doing, because most of the time they're too wrapped up in the work or too bashful to tell anyone themselves.

This reminds me of someone like Dennis Johnson on the great Celtics teams of the 1980's (in stark contrast to Dennis Johnson when he was with the Supersonics and the Suns, where he was largely considered a selfish player). The Boston "Big Three" of Bird, Parrish and McHale dominated the stat sheets and the headlines, but it was always "DJ" who guarded the other team's best guard or small forward – DJ defended guys like Magic Johnson, Andrew Toney, Isaiah Thomas, and Michael Jordan. DJ was the epitome of an unsung hero on those great Celtics teams.

In the end, Dennis Johnson made the Basketball Hall of Fame. He was that good of a defender and team player. But he's almost an afterthought of those great Celtics teams, and it's partly because he swallowed his pride and took a back seat to the "Big Three."

The implementer is a good person and a great worker, but most of the time, the implementer takes a back seat. There is nothing wrong with being an implementer, especially if you're starting out in your career and you are working closely with your boss or other co-workers that will recognize your contribution. But if you want to work from home and do so effectively, you have to be more like Abe Lincoln.

ABE LINCOLN

This is the rare breed (notice Shaw used Lincoln – not exactly a run-of-the-mill President) that does a job above and beyond the call of duty and then tells everyone about it. So you are combining the best qualities of the showman – the ability to talk, and the implementer – the ability to get the job done.

Striving to be the "Abe Lincoln" is even more essential for a remote employee than an office worker. As a remote worker, you're not top of mind all the time (since you're not physically in the office), and you may not get recognition for tasks you complete, especially if you don't speak up about it.

This happened to me a couple of times earlier in my career (while I was working in an office setting), and I've learned that there are people you can trust and people you cannot trust. The ones you can't trust you still have to work with. Just don't let them steal your thunder. You need to be willing to say to the world / your boss / your customer / your co-workers, "hey, guys! Take a look at what I did!" As long as you do that, you won't allow others the opportunity to take credit for your good work.

Think of someone like Magic Johnson or Moses Malone. Magic could talk the talk – but he could also walk the walk and he was one of the best five players in the history of the NBA. Magic still talks a good game. And he's continued to back up his talk, currently as an outstanding businessman and now as part owner of the Los Angeles Dodgers.

Malone, hall-of-fame basketball player who went to the NBA right out of high school back when that jump was considered impossible, famously predicted a playoff sweep in the 1983 playoffs. In an interview at the end of the regular season, a reporter asked Malone to predict the outcome of the playoffs. His answer? "Fo – Fo – Fo." What he meant was that the Sixers would sweep the conference semifinals 4-0, the conference finals, 4-0 and then sweep the NBA Finals 4-0. A playoff record 12-0 is what Malone was predicting.

Malone was the MVP of the league in 1983. So he could certainly back up his talk with outstanding play. The outcome? The Sixers did lose one game to the Bucks in the conference finals but won all the rest of their games that year, for a 12-1 playoff record. And Moses Malone was named Finals MVP.

Malone and Magic are two examples of the Abe Lincoln persona in practice. Both were great players, and both let their opponents and the fans know that they were great players. Nobody would ever say that Magic and Malone talked a better game than what they showed on the court. They were both great and they told people about it – and the "walk" and "talk" were in balance. That's the essence of the Abe Lincoln persona.

GIVE CREDIT STRATEGICALLY

You may run into a situation at work where you have to give praise and/or credit to someone who didn't do the work. And that may be the right move.

Perhaps the project is going really badly, and it's mostly one teammate's fault. Suddenly something good happens! Maybe you actually hit a deadline or the project gets back on track as the result of your effort and the hard work of your team. In this situation, it may be beneficial to your team, the customer, and ultimately you, if you give credit to your teammates, especially the teammate that has been struggling.

I only do this if I like my team! But when I do like my team, and especially when I feel like they could use the morale boost, I will freely give them credit for whatever good work we accomplished.

This method of positive reinforcement creates a self-fulfilling virtuous cycle. When the struggling teammate realizes he's being praised, he likes that feeling. He then will want to do more things to get more credit, so he can maintain that feeling. Suddenly the struggling teammate becomes a solid contributor to the team.

I have seen this phenomenon happen time and again during high-pressure projects. Some people struggle with tight timelines, and panic when customers have high expectations. Some weaker team members will retreat into a shell, and if you don't give them support, you could lose them as productive team members.

So when you get into a situation where teammates are struggling, give them some love. Tell them "good job" and lend your support, and stick up for them in front of the customer or other project team members. Your support will energize them and allow them to do better work.

And when they do better work, your entire team looks better. If you can accomplish all this from the comfort of your own home, that's even better. Now you have established that you can run an effective team from home.

Take the blame

Although not specifically mentioned in Shaw's article, it can't be ignored that if something goes badly and you're in charge, take the blame. As the project lead, you need to take the blame 100% of the time. This is a non-negotiable point. There is nothing worse than a leader who makes excuses.

I can't tell you how many times I've said, "oh yeah, that's my fault. I should have been all over that," or something to that effect. Especially when you're leading a distributed or remote team, I find it's essential to take blame when something goes wrong. If not, you alienate the team, and you may actually look worse to your customer.

You never want the customer to say, "Boy, I know it wasn't all Joe's work that was responsible for this major blunder, but did you see how quickly he threw his team under the bus? That's unprofessional. I would never want to work with someone like that."

And you know what happens next? The project fails, or the project ends, and you quietly get shown the door.

I have never been in a situation where taking the blame was a bad idea. I have never been thrown out of a project or office or company for taking the blame for something (I've come close, but it's never actually happened). There's something endearing and honest about taking a bullet and taking the blame and not passing the buck. As our 33rd President Harry S. Truman would say, "the buck stops here."

Customers and clients know that at some point, a project will go badly. It may only be temporary, it may just be a minor hiccup, or it may be catastrophic. Regardless, the way you handle yourself during the fire drill matters. The way you phrase email messages matters. If you're under the gun and it's your project, take the bullet. It will benefit you more than harm you in the long run. It has for me.

The follow-up to taking the blame: gather the information that caused the error, get to the root cause, and solve the problem. Problem-solving skills are essential in project work, mostly because projects are wrought with problems.

WHETHER SHOWERING PRAISE OR TAKING BLAME – IT STILL HAS TO BE ON YOUR SCHEDULE

Sometimes when you're in the depths of despair during a project, you have all-nighters and you work weekends. It's not uncommon and it is not 100% unavoidable. Regardless of your actual work schedule, you should communicate your progress (Abe Lincoln), praise, and take blame on your schedule, just as you laid out in your unofficial SLA.

Weekly status meetings are best for progress updates and praise. The project may require daily updates if there's blood in the streets and the project is nose-diving uncontrollably (and yes I know I mixed metaphors, I think it still works). Either way, set up guidelines to determine when communication will be sent out and when you will host conference calls.

If you don't establish (what I've heard called) a "cadence" for status calls, whether daily, weekly (I've actually had hourly during crunch time), you will spend all of your time dealing with communicating status, and not enough time actually doing the good work it takes to successfully finish a project.

I've found the following outline very helpful when determining weekly status meeting content. I've created weekly status documents with the following sections:

- *PROJECT PLAN REVIEW:* this is typically where you take blame. You also need to ensure you're on top of all the moving parts of the plan. If you're the lead, you own the plan, no matter what the official "RACI" says.

- *ACTION ITEMS FROM PREVIOUS STATUS UPDATES:* this is where you channel Abe Lincoln and/or shower praise on your team and/or the project team.

- *CURRENT STATUS OF DELIVERABLES:* here is where you may want to show your work (Abe Lincoln), or better yet, allow one of your hardworking teammates to show her work for a current deliverable. It will show the customer that she is a good worker and she's progressing nicely with her task.

- *UPDATE ON ANY ADVANCED CONFIGURATION AND/OR CUSTOM-IZATION OR "HARD STUFF" THAT NEEDS TO BE COMPLETED:* often during projects there's that one requirement that is unique to the customer and does not fit inside your product "out of the box." You then need to enlist someone on the product development team or the advanced configuration team to work on this item. Hopefully these items are few and far between, because this area is where projects fall apart.

- **NEXT STEPS:** very important to communicate and agree on next steps. Otherwise you will need a status meeting every 15 minutes.

- **NEXT TIME ON SITE:** I will get to this in much more detail in the next section called "Showing your Face." This is important to communicate as well in advance as possible. Especially if you are bringing in some other resources, e.g. specialist or an executive, it's critical you let your customer know early. Customers don't like to be surprised.

- **TECHNICAL TOPICS:** any technical issues and/or challenges that need to be specifically discussed. This is a good way for you to figure out ahead of time what resources you may need to line up to solve any technical issues.

- **PREVIOUSLY UNIDENTIFIED TOPICS:** this is an important topic that will allow both the customer and your team to voice any concerns, issues or other general information that needs to be tracked. Typically, someone will bring up a topic that was previously missed but is critical to a successful project completion. It is now your responsibility to take that issue and (hopefully quickly) solve it. It is also your responsibility to put that issue on the list for "Action Items from Previous Status Updates" (the 2nd section of this list). If you don't do that, you look like you're not following up, you're not being proactive, and you're not paying attention. Don't be that person.

- *MEETING NOTES:* any notes you need to take during the meeting can go either in the sections directly or in the meeting notes at the end of the document.

This format has worked wonders for me. It creates structure around meetings and the "Previously Unidentified Topics" section allows for anything we missed, which is critical. You don't want anyone leaving the status meeting thinking, "Oh I can't believe we didn't talk about the fact that Joe's shirt has been untucked the entire week." By allowing "Previously Unidentified Topics" to be raised, it eliminates the ambiguity.

Most importantly, it ensures everyone is on the same page. The customer, the project team, and any other stakeholders are all in alignment. If the steering committee or executive sponsor needs an update, you can simply turn over the most recent status meeting document. And if they can't figure it out, well, that's a topic for another book.

PART 3

SHOWING YOUR FACE – DON'T ALWAYS WORK FROM HOME

My Uncle Ken is a mathematical genius. He graduated top of his class from Merrimack College in 1968 with a mathematics degree and went to work for the government as a civilian. Over his long and successful career, he and his family (my Aunt Sue, and their children Eddie and Anne-Marie) traveled the world, living in Iowa, Florida, Germany, Alabama, and Washington DC.

He and my Aunt Sue are now retired in Colorado, but he still does consulting work on the side because he's in such high demand. He's met heads of state and has worked in the Pentagon. He calls Condoleezza Rice "Condi." There's even a family rumor – started by my father –he was involved in the bombing of Libya and Muammar Gaddafi in 1986.

My Uncle Ken knows what he's talking about. His intelligence oozes out of him when he speaks, and he routinely describes interactions with less intelligent people in the world, usually with an equal degree of disdain and enjoyment.

He rarely gives me advice, but when he does it's precious. When I started working at EY in 2011, he asked me about the job. I told him that I would be primarily working from home. He said, "make sure to show your face in the office every once in a while. If they don't know who you are, it's much easier for them to fire you." I took my uncle's advice seriously and have continued the notion of "showing my face" ever since. This may seem counterintuitive for the reader, since this is a book about working from home effectively.

The concept of "showing your face" in a physical office is still really important today. With the advanced remote work technology available – web meetings, join.me, Google hangouts, and others – actually going into the office may not be as important in the future. I would be surprised if companies had multiple physical offices in the future. But for now, following my uncle's advice is a good idea.

"Showing your face" has other advantages. You also need to

build your network, not just for your own benefit but also for the benefit of others. By physically seeing a co-worker, shaking a hand exchanging a warm smile or a laugh, you have made a connection.

Human connection is still what drives the business world, even though it doesn't appear that way since many Millennials constantly have their faces stuffed into their cell phones. You are more apt to buy from someone you like. You are more willing to help someone you know. Technology is allowing us to virtually connect with others in new and exciting ways, but especially for the generations that didn't grow up with this technology, nothing replaces a handshake and a smile.

Growing your network is more important now than ever before in human history. Five thousand years ago, you only interacted with your tribe, and you were limited to the knowledge and relationships that were established within your small community. Five hundred years ago, you were limited to your village or sect or township, and many folks were tied to their landowner's property. Today, you can interact with someone across the world in real time. You can shoot a video in Long Island that kids from the Fiji Islands can view instantaneously. You can now connect with anyone that has a cell phone signal or a wireless device.

Growing and nurturing your network will drive your career progression. The more people you know, the better off you will be. The more contacts you can acquire and maintain, the more "loose ties" you will have, which may help you or it may help the people connected to you. You never know who in your network may tap you for information or advice. But having a strong network is an absolute necessity in today's working world.

So what does this have to do with working from home effectively? Two things: one is that you cannot work from home all the time, and second is you cannot work in a vacuum, even if you primarily work remotely.

Working from home all the time limits your chances to build a network. If you are a full-time at-home worker, there are other ways to connect with people in your community or in your industry. You could join a community group or you could volunteer. You could join discussion groups on LinkedIn or subscribe and contribute to niche blogs that discuss your business. You could show up at a "Meet-up" and find others in your area with common interests. You could become involved in your church. But it's critical that you get out of the house some of the time. Working in a vacuum and never interacting with the other humans is no way to go through life. You are not a pod – you're a capable human being that people want to see.

So what have we learned in part three? Hopefully you got these key takeaways:

- **THERE IS NO SUCH THING AS A "BEST PRACTICE."** Anyone that tells you otherwise is lying to you. Thought leaders ask good questions, they don't have all the answers. There's nothing wrong with trying different ways to get things done. The way I work at home may not be the way you want to work at home, and that's fine. What I do is best for me – you have to find what's best for you.

- **CREATING AND FOLLOWING A MORNING ROUTINE** is a method that has worked really well for me and gets me ready to attack the day. I'm in a good frame of mind to focus on work, and the routines I've developed have become habits, so it doesn't feel like a huge effort. Going to the gym in the morning, for example, is now just part of my day. And if I can move some weights and myself around in the morning, I'm better equipped to deal with the challenges of the workday.

- **SETTING BOUNDARIES** is essential for the remote worker. If you do not set boundaries, your boss or your customer will do it for you, which means you may be working at the crack of dawn, until midnight and on the weekends. Don't let others set your boundaries. Instead communicate your working schedule clearly and stick to it. This is the way to achieve true work/life balance.

- **DON'T ALWAYS WORK FROM HOME.** Whether it's an occasional office visit, an on-site trip to a customer or prospect, or meeting a co-worker for a coffee or a beer, make it a priority to not hole yourself up in your house. Remember the other humans. As George Costanza famously quipped, "we're living in a society!"

As we wind down Part Three, take a moment and decide what you want your working life to be like. Do you want people interrupting you during your family dinner? Do you want your day to feel haphazard and riddled with disorganization? Or do you want to take control of the situation? The choice is yours.

Now we're on to Part Four, where I will tell you a little bit about the underbelly of working from home. Some benefits that you may not consider as you sit at your office cubicle. Let me give you a sneak-peak into some non-obvious benefits of the work-at-home life.

PART 4

NON-OBVIOUS BENEFITS
OF WORKING FROM HOME

PEGGY: "You have a garbage disposal in your bathtub?"

KRAMER: "Oh, yeah, and I use it all the time. Yeah, I made this whole meal in there."

ELAINE: "This food was in the shower with you?"

KRAMER: "Mm-hmm. I prepared it as I bathed."

- SEINFELD: THE APOLOGY, EPISODE 165

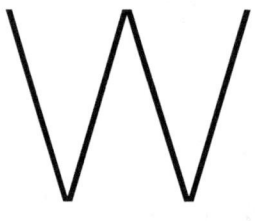orking at home is great for a number of reasons, many of which we've covered in the previous sections. This section is dedicated to the subtle things that make working at home a true pleasure.

Part four is meant to be a bit lighter than some of the other topics we've covered, but in many ways I am more grateful for some of the items I chose in Part four than I am for any of the other topics I previously mentioned.

PART 4

YOU HAVE YOUR OWN BATHROOM

There is a scene in an early Seinfeld episode called "The Busboy" where Jerry is quizzing George as to where the best public restrooms are in New York City. Jerry gives an address and George quickly rattles off the best available option:

JERRY: Anywhere in the city?

GEORGE: Anywhere in the city - I'll tell you the best public toilet.

JERRY: Okay – Fifty-fourth and Sixth?

GEORGE: Sperry Rand Building – 14th floor, Morgan Apparel. Mention my name - she'll give you the key.

JERRY: Alright, Sixty-fifth and Tenth.

GEORGE: (Scoffs) Are you kidding? Lincoln Center. Alice Tully Hall, the Met. Magnificent facilities.

In real life, you will run into situations at work where you have to use a bathroom that does not have the George Constanza seal of approval. You may work in an old office building where the bathrooms haven't been renovated in a while. They may be drafty. They may not be very clean. You may have to use a stall right next to another guy using a stall – a more uncomfortable predicament I cannot imagine.

When I was working at Putnam Investments in downtown Boston, I consistently walked into the bathroom and it was unusable. Without getting into gruesome details, there must have been a water buffalo that was cleaning himself in there on a daily basis. If I had to "sit down," I would either have to find another bathroom on a different floor, hold it, or go out to a neighboring hotel and test my luck with the lobby bathroom. It was a hellish situation.

When I'm home, I have access to my own bathroom, the one that only my wife and I use. It's clean. It's usually very neat. There is always a supply of whatever paper products are needed. I can flit in and out of the bathroom without a care in the world. It's a delight.

When you're working from home, it's the little things like all-day access to your own bathroom that make the experience that much more enjoyable.

PART 4

FLEXIBLE SHOWER SCHEDULE

n addition to using your own bathroom whenever you want, you may also leverage the flexibility of the "anytime shower." The anytime shower is crucial for my work-at-home schedule. There are many days I shower early in the morning. Some other days I like to shower right before or after lunch. If I have lots of crazy errands to run or yard work to do or other tasks, I may not shower until after work.

The flexible shower schedule is only available if you're working at home. Unfortunately, the mores that pervade today's society demand we shower before going into the office. It doesn't matter that we are slowly killing ourselves by not walking or standing enough, sitting too much, and eating crappy carb-loaded food all day. As long as we're showered, we're accepted.

Working from home affords you the capability to do things like taking a walk or going for a run in the morning. Maybe you choose to do some work around the house or in the yard during lunch or during a mid-afternoon lull in your schedule. And you may want to go to the gym right after work, or maybe hit a bucket of golf balls or play nine holes. None of these activities require a shower.

So embrace your smelly side and shower when you want to shower. I'm writing this paragraph at 9:52AM and I have not showered yet, but I've already walked almost 6 miles, gone to the gym, checked my email, read a few blog posts and had breakfast. Maybe I'll shower at lunchtime.

PART 4

YOU CAN TAKE A NAP

Steven Kotler writes about "flow", or the state of maximum awareness where your subconscious mind has taken over the conscious mind, and you are hyper-productive. The flow state is fleeting and highly creative people are always looking for ways to get into flow.

It turns out that there are ways to deconstruct how to get into a flow state, which Kotler explains in his book "The Rise of Superman." What Kotler also mentions is that after an intense period of flow state, your body and mind are shot. You need to relax and reboot. In many cases, you need a nap.

Taking a nap during the workday is impossible when you're in a traditional office setting. Some innovative companies like Google now allow their workers to nap in "pods" during the day, but the vast majority of corporate America asks their workers to come in early, leave late, disrupting sleeping patterns along the way by feeding them caffeine.

At home, you can take a nap whenever you want. If you know you have to really focus on a problem during the morning hours, you may want to block off 30 minutes on your calendar in the early afternoon to decompress and allow your brain to recover from being in a hyperactive "flow" state. Just block off your calendar, turn off the ringer on your phone, close the door, draw the shades and close your eyes. I have a futon in my office that's a great place to nap. After 30 minutes, even if I don't fall totally asleep, I feel relaxed and rejuvenated.

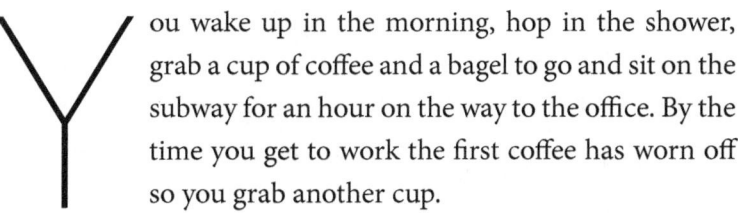

PART 4

YOU CAN CONTROL
YOUR DIET

Y ou wake up in the morning, hop in the shower, grab a cup of coffee and a bagel to go and sit on the subway for an hour on the way to the office. By the time you get to work the first coffee has worn off so you grab another cup.

Now it's mid-morning and those donuts in the break room aren't going to eat themselves, so you dig in.

Thankfully noontime rolls around, but you're stuck in a "work through lunch" meeting. They've brought in deli sandwiches and bags of potato chips and no other options, so you partake.

After lunch, you grab a diet soda to avoid the sugar crash of all the processed carbs you've stuffed your face with all day. Then it's the 4:00PM doldrums, which hit you like a brick. Luckily it's Peggy's birthday and someone made cupcakes, so you jam that sugar ball into your mouth.

The 5:00PM bell hits and you head home, arrive at 6:00PM to a great meal of spaghetti and meatballs. You crack two Bud Lights, guzzle those down and call it a night around 11:00PM.

Does this sound familiar? If it does, you are going to have health problems your entire life, which may not be too much longer. Sadly, this routine (or a variation of it) is all too common in today's workplace. And the office setting perpetuates it.

Because you're rushing out the door in the morning, you don't have time to make breakfast, or drink some water. You opt for the quick-and-easy bagel. Because you're at the office, the only option is the sandwich and chips. And because your husband was home all day with the kids, your only option is the quick-and-easy spaghetti he was able to cobble together while you were at work.

When I work from home, I make the vast majority of my meals. The meals I don't make, I get down at the local diner, where all my meals are made custom for me, with the ingredients I want, and without the ingredients I don't. I control every aspect of the food that I eat, from the portion to the content to the timing. As a result, my diet is exactly what I want it to be.

Contrast the above nightmarish daily diet with what I typically eat:

- **PROTEIN POWER** mixed with water within 15 minutes of waking

- **BREAKFAST:** Eggs with veggies and beans if home or eggs with veggies and chicken if at the diner. At least 4 glasses of water and 3 cups of coffee

- **LUNCH:** Protein with veggies and either lentils or beans if home or protein with veggies at the diner. At least 3 glasses of water

- **SNACK (SOMETIMES):** Greek yogurt with walnuts and blueberries or a kale shake

- **DINNER:** protein with veggies and either lentils or beans if home or protein and veggies if we go out for dinner. At least 2 glasses of water and usually 2 glasses of beer.

- **AFTER DINNER:** herbal tea and dark chocolate (occasionally as a treat)

I have a difficult time sticking to this diet on the road. The times I am on the road, I notice that my diet is not quite as good as when I'm home. I still know what foods to avoid, but sometimes I cave and grab a diet soda or a granola bar because it's convenient and I'm in a weakened emotional state from traveling.

The times I work from home I can control everything. And I also find it's much easier to stick to my meal plan. Over the past ten years, I've probably saved myself 15 pounds of belly fat and lots of sleepless nights because I'm able to control my diet.

Hopefully you get the gist – you can benefit greatly from working at home, and not just in the ways you'd expect. My whole day is better just from having access to my own bathroom.

In our last section, Part Five, we'll discuss some tricks I've learned over the years to keep your work-at-home situation razor sharp. I'll also show you some things to avoid – like meetings.

PART 5

TIPS, TRICKS & TRAPS TO WORK FROM HOME EFFECTIVELY

GEORGE:	"Jerry, look at my eyes."
JERRY:	"A little less beady today."
GEORGE:	"Because I'm refreshed! I finally found a way to sleep at the office. Under my desk. I lie on my back. I tuck in the chair. I'm invisible."

- SEINFELD: THE NAP, EPISODE 152

PART 5

KEEP CALENDAR
UP-TO-DATE

Your calendar can be your best friend or your worst enemy, to paraphrase Chip Douglas (Jim Carey's character) in "Cable Guy". If you manage your calendar well, you can free yourself from horrible time-sucking meetings, you can shape your day based on the times of day you're most effective, and you can "channel in the good, block out the bad" as Kevin Nealon would say in "Happy Gilmore."

The best way to keep your calendar is by being proactive about it. When you look at your week, you should block out time for the following:

- Travel

- Meals

- Concentration Time / Thinking Blocks

- Breaks

I worked with a very effective manager at Tidemark who always blocked off his calendar from 5:00PM to 8:00PM on Friday nights. Why? Tidemark was a California-based company, and this manager was based on the East coast. He had a wife and a family, and he didn't want some jackass in Redwood City to schedule a Friday meeting at 3:00PM Pacific, which was right as he was about to take his wife to dinner at 6:00PM Eastern time. So he set up a recurring weekly meeting that blocked off his calendar and ensured his Friday nights were spent with his family instead of on a pointless conference call. Brilliant idea!

PART 5

TRAVEL TIME

f you have to go into the office, or fly on an airplane somewhere or meet a customer or client, add that travel time to
your calendar. That way, nobody can schedule a meeting
during your travel time. I fight fiercely to keep my travel time
my time, so I can focus on doing the things I want to do while
I'm on the road.

For example, I may have a few things to review for the customer
I'm going to visit. Reviewing that information on the plane may
make the difference between me being prepared for the meeting or sounding like a jackass in front of the CFO.

I also may just want to relax when I'm on the plane. Let's say
I already prepared extensively for my meeting, and I feel con-

fident about my preparation and our chances of doing well in front of the executives. Many times I will keep the laptop closed on the plane, and I'll concentrate on the book I'm reading, especially if it's a non-fiction book.

I can't tell you how many times I've read something on the plane that was so insightful I used a tool from the book in a meeting later that day or later in the week. When I'm concentrating on the book, I forget what I have to focus on for my meeting, which allows my mind to wander and "connect the dots." I highly encourage you to read a good non-fiction book – business, biography, or sports – when you're traveling. Even if you don't get a tool to use in the meeting, you may just feel more like an elite athlete or a CEO if you read about high-performing individuals. Your confidence will surge.

I still remember once, on the plane before a meeting, reading an autobiography by John Wooden, one of the best college basketball coaches of all time. I was so fired up when I got off that plane I could have run through a wall! The book was called "My Personal Best" if you want to pick it up -- it's a classic manual on excellence, both on and off the court. As for the meeting? We nailed it, and we ultimately won the business.

PART 5

MEALS

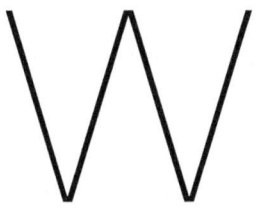

Without the proper nutrition and the right amount of time to eat, you will be operating at suboptimal capacity, no matter how hard you're working and how much you think you're getting done.

What is proper nutrition? The answer is different for everyone, and it does depend on your body type, your genetic predisposition to certain conditions like obesity and diabetes, and other factors. As a baseline, though, you can get some benefit from following a diet that is heavy on whole foods and light on processed foods. You don't have to do a Paleo diet, or an Atkins diet, or a South Beach diet, but you should be paying attention to the ingredients in the foods that you eat. If there are two options, and one is organic and the other is not, pick the organic option. There have been tons of studies done on the benefit of eating organic food, and the detriment of eating food that's either been genetically modified or raised in an industrial fashion.

A perfect example is beef. People have been eating meat for thousands of years, and up until recently were not getting fat or having gastrointestinal issues like Irritable Bowel Syndrome (IBS). Within the last fifty years, these conditions have skyrocketed in the North American population, which coincides all too conveniently with the advent of the industrial farm. In today's big farms, cows typically eat corn – which they cannot physically digest, but which causes them to gain more weight – and they remain in and around their trough for most of the day. This means the cows are confined, they get little to no exercise, and they stomp around in their own feces. These cows, who are deprived of a regular cow diet – grass – develop all sorts of ailments, which are "cured" by injecting these cows with medicine.

Then those cows are slaughtered and sold to you. Who knows what impact eating that cow will have on you? Do you know what medicine the cow received? You do know that it probably had digestive issues from being fed corn, which could lead to problems solved only by chemists in Monsanto labs.

Grass-fed cows that are allowed to graze the way cows are supposed to graze have hardly any digestive issues and are generally much healthier throughout their lifecycle. Their digestive track is healthy, which means their gut is in balance and does not require outside chemical intervention. Their meat is more expensive, but it is worth it. Trust me, skip the Starbucks coffee, make a pot at home and enjoy organic grass-fed beef instead. Your gut will thank you.

Don't take my word on this – there are several good books out recently that explore gut health and its relationship to the food we eat. Two books I recommend are "Gut" by Guilia Enders and "The Mind-Gut Connection" by Dr. Emeran Mayer. Both talk extensively about how you can choose better foods for your overall health, not just your gut health.

Having enough time to eat is also essential. According to Charles Poliquin, master strength trainer and founder of strengthsensei. com, fat people chew their food an average of 17 times before swallowing, and fit people chew an average of 45 times. In order for you to slow down and eat your food at the proper pace – slowly – you need to allot enough time to the endeavor.

So do yourself a favor and block off your calendar for lunch, and enjoy that Greek salad with organic flank steak.

PART 5

PLAY JAZZ OR
CLASSICAL MUSIC

f you're in a loud environment, like if you share a small apartment w/ your wife who also works from home, you may need to play some music. When my wife and I were living in New York City, we rented a beautiful apartment in the West Village. It was newly-renovated and in the perfect location – right on the corner of Washington Street and West 10th Street. Our block was nice and quiet, but just a block away, the craziness of the Village beckoned.

The problem was that the apartment was only 800 square feet. When we both worked from home, this became a problem, especially if we both had meetings at the same time. I took many conference calls from the bathroom and the hallway. When she had a meeting and I didn't, it was even worse for me because I couldn't concentrate. So I routinely went to Spotify or Pandora and put on either classical or jazz music – something without words.

For me, and this is different for everyone, when I hear music with lyrics, I start humming or singing the lyrics to myself, and I lose concentration. If I listen to jazz, though, I can sometimes get into a deeper level of concentration – almost getting into the "flow" state that Mihaly Csikszentmihalyi talks about in his books and TED talks, and what Kotler describes (mentioned previously). Listening to jazz also sometimes spurs my creativity, and I can look at a problem in a new way – it gets a different part of my brain going.

I suggest jazz and/or classical as opposed to white noise, which doesn't give me the sudden weird burst of creativity I get from listening to jazz or classical. This creativity burst has happened to me several times and I really enjoy when it happens.

PART 5

SAY "NO" TO MEETINGS

How many times have you greeted a co-worker or business associate and asked them how they were and they replied back with "busy! I'm so busy."? In today's always-on, interconnected world, it seems people are busier than ever. It's even become a badge of honor at the workplace to talk about how busy you are, how late you worked the night before, how little sleep you get, how you ate dinner at a gas station.

I find this behavior appalling. Do you know what you're telling people when you say you're busy? You're telling the world that you have no control over your work schedule or your work life. None. Why are you so busy all the time? Can't you get your act together?

I offer a quick-and-dirty solution. Say "no" to more meetings. I know if you work in a corporate environment you probably can't say "no" to every meeting – although you may want to decline all of them. But if you habitually say "yes" to every single meeting request that comes across your email inbox, you are effectively saying that the person sending the meeting request deserves your time more than you deserve your time.

In some cases, it may be completely legitimate to remove yourself from a meeting. You may not need to be present for the meeting – you only need to gather a few action items afterwards. If you consistently notice that meeting organizers tend to send out requests when a task list will do, kindly respond that you will not make their meeting. Instead, please send along the task list with your deliverables. That way you still get your tasks, the organizer feels important because he's put a meeting together, and you get your time back to focus on more important matters – like doing some real work.

Meetings are the antithesis of work. They drain productivity and are generally pointless. How many times have you attended a meeting with no agenda? If the meeting organizer doesn't provide an agenda, what he's saying is that he can't even be bothered enough to tell you what the meeting is about, but he "requires" your attendance. If that is the case – unless it's the CEO or a key investor in your company – you can easily decline the meeting, since you have no agenda, and therefore no objective, which means the meeting owner is advertising ahead of time that the meeting is a waste of time.

Do yourself a favor and take a closer look at a meeting invite before you say yes. Does it have an agenda? Is there a clear reason why you should attend? Is this meeting the best use of your time? Can you find an alternative – like getting a task list after the meeting ends? Be more critical of every invite that comes your way – just because you're flattered you are being considered for a meeting doesn't mean you are obligated to attend.

Nancy Reagan's War on Drugs was ridiculous, and it was never going to work. But if you steal her slogan – "Just say no", and apply that to your meeting invites, you will quickly find time that you never knew you had. The end result is you have more time for yourself, which means you won't be constantly busy. You may actually get eight hours of sleep. You sit down and eat dinner with your friends or your family. You may even get a chance to read a book.

PART 5

CHECKLISTS

confess I used to be really bad at getting things done. I would procrastinate, and then I would procrastinate some more, and then with the deadline fast-approaching, I would cram and produce a reasonable facsimile of my deliverable. I handed over a ton of terrible work early in my career.

What I realized somewhere along the line is that I was behaving based on a feeling of being overwhelmed. If I had four or five things to get done, I wouldn't know where to start, and I would freak out and not do anything. Then when it was time to hand in an assignment or file a report, I would whip up some extemporaneous nonsense and pass it off as a professional representation of myself.

Now I use checklists. It can be very simple – most of the time

I just write down my list on a piece of paper, or an index card. And then I check off things as I go, and only work on one thing at a time. Funny thing about working on one thing at a time: you actually work more deliberately because you're not distracted by the other things on your list. You have time to focus and really understand the problem you're trying to solve. And you actually gain time because your first attempt/draft is so much better than it would be if you were a scatterbrained multitasker.

Checklists sound stupid, and they sound pointless. That's what I used to think anyway. Now I live by them. I've even had checklists of checklists. I can't stop. They're amazing. Try it.

PART 5

TAKE BREAKS

uild them into your day. Walking is a great way to take a break. You may just want to relax for a few minutes and that's OK too. Think of it as your "remote water cooler time." I've worked in offices where people are so unproductive and ineffective because they spend the majority of their time flapping their gums to their co-workers nearby, and when they're not yammering away at their cubicle they're literally hanging around the kitchen looking for someone who will listen to their gibberish. So don't worry about taking a quick break at home. You're still doing better than most people in the office.

As a matter of fact, many studies have shown that if you take breaks periodically you are more productive overall. The brain can only focus for so long, and then you get into a haze, and you're not really concentrating anymore. By taking a break, you're recharging your brain's batteries and allowing it to relax. How many times have you thought of something in the shower or in your sleep? Why do you think that is? It's because your brain is relaxed, and you are letting your thoughts flow. If you're stuck in front of your laptop for hours on end, you lose the ability to think creatively – but you can get that ability back by stepping away for a few minutes.

Going outside for a walk is specifically good for you. You get the blood moving around and hopefully you get to feel the sun on your face. That's a good feeling and if you trap yourself in your home office all day, you won't ever see the sun, which is really sad. That great big ball in the sky has positive psychological effects. Why do you think rainy climates have more cases of depression? So get out on the grass, or walk down the sidewalk in your city, or go to a park. Let the sun hit your face, even for just a few minutes. You'll get a hit of vitamin D and you'll also experience a feeling of glee. It's worth it.

Other great options for breaks:

- **MOBILITY BREAK:** Kelly Starrett talks about this in "Deskbound", his excellent tome. Essentially you allow your body to get into positions that it naturally should be in all the time, but you need to work on these positions because we're a lazy culture with horrible habits. Something like doing a five-minute squat is a revelation.

- **STRETCHING BREAK:** similar to a mobility break, just stretching your legs and torso a bit after a period of focus will activate your muscles, will get your blood flowing and will jumpstart you back into a more active state.

- *LAYING ON THE GROUND:* stretch out your arms and legs and just lay on the ground. This is a great way to take the pressure off your bones and your joints for a few minutes and relax. You can do some deep breathing if you'd like too. It doesn't take too much time before you feel a rush of relaxation.

- *HAVE A WORK AREA AND A SLEEP AREA* – and never the two shall meet

- *TECHNOLOGY:* If you read any of Arianna Huffington's work, she is a big proponent of keeping the sleeping area free from technology. I rely on my cell phone as my alarm clock, so I'm not totally following her guidelines, but I do think it's important to keep your work and your sleep separated. The poet laureate Notorious B.I.G. once said, "keep your family and business completely separated." Yes, he was talking about running a crack cocaine business, and perhaps his rule is more important in that line of work than in software sales. But still, the rule applies for me, too. I keep all work-related communication out of the bedroom. I do that by following a few simple steps:

- *I SET UP MY PHONE WITH A "DO NOT DISTURB"* from 9:00PM – 7:00AM. I've set up my wife as a "VIP" contact in my phone, so she can call me during that window and it will bypass the "do not disturb" setting. This comes in handy when we're both traveling and she calls me late at night when she forgets the time zone difference. More importantly, the "do not disturb" setting acts as a screening mechanism for me, and allows me to sleep soundly. Especially when I'm traveling to a different time zone, the "do not disturb" setting becomes essential. Many times if I'm on the West Coast, a colleague or friend or family member will call me at 9:00AM Eastern time. It's not their fault, they don't all know my travel schedule. But it's 6:00AM for me, and I'm most likely still sleeping. Waking up to the sound of a text message or phone ringing is a horrible way to start the day. I've had bouts of anger as a result. So now, with the "do not disturb" setting, I'm sleeping until 6:30AM no matter what coast I'm on, and I wake up feeling good because I'm waking up when I want to, not when someone thinks it's convenient for them.

You can go more covert than the "do not disturb" setting and set your phone to airplane mode. Or you can completely remove the phone from your bedroom, and use a traditional alarm clock. I opt for the "do not disturb" because of the VIP override feature. If my wife really needs to get a hold of me I want her to be able to do that. But the airplane mode works great, too, if you want to completely block out communication. And the best way to ensure you don't get interrupted during a night's sleep is to keep the phone out of the room or turn it off completely. Younger, less married folks than me can get away with these options.

- **CHECKING EMAIL:** I don't check email after I get into my bedroom. Checking email "one last time" is a convenient little trap that many people – including my wife – fall into. You are just about ready to turn off the lights, and you decide to check your email before bed. Bam! A big email comes through from your boss/client/customer/colleague/HR department that is marked extra urgent, requiring your attention right away. You get out of bed, fire up your laptop and diligently respond, taking into consideration all the important points you need to summon from your sleepy brain. And now you're up for the next four hours, thinking about the email, your response, and all the implications and permutations of the situation. This is no way to go through life. Set a limit and do not check email once you reach the bedroom. Your psyche and your body will thank you.

- *NO TELEVISION IN THE BEDROOM.* I actually can't believe that I'm in favor of this one. My wife is very anti-TV-in-the-bedroom, and since we've been living together – 2012 – we have not had a TV in the bedroom. I used to fall asleep to the TV on nightly, setting the sleep alarm on the set to turn off right after I shut down. When we first moved in together, I was nervous about being able to fall asleep without the white noise of ESPN on low volume. Enter a white noise maker. Whether an app on your phone, a dull fan in the room or an air conditioning unit in the window, white noise works much better than SportsCenter. I once was a sleep-timer TV junkie, and now I'm a convert. Many studies have shown that watching a screen – TV, phone, laptop – will keep your mind in "awake" mode, which will hurt your sleep. You won't fall asleep as easily and you won't have deep enough sleep. Lack of sleep and lack of deep sleep – a full sleep cycle – can cause all sorts of problems, including chronic fatigue and potentially other brain-related illnesses like Parkinson's and Alzeimer's.

There are other, more aggressive measures you can take to ensure you don't consume any tech before bed. Some people refuse to read any Kindle or iPad device and will only read physi-cal books. I enjoy a physical book but it's not a requirement for bedtime reading.

No matter how extreme or benevolent you decide to approach removing tech from the bedroom, just remember that you're saving yourself by doing so, and you're allowing your needs to trump the needs of others. I'm sure your boss would love to call you at all hours of the night to ensure that his hair-brained idea is being executed. But you need your sleep, and you need to dis-connect from the workday and transition into the nighttime, re-laxing hours. You should be free from work thoughts as you get ready for bed and then ultimately get a good night's sleep. Don't let someone else dictate when you get your rest. Which leads me to my next point: get at least eight hours of sleep per night.

PART 5

SLEEP 8 HOURS PER NIGHT

JERRY: Hey everybody, I'm on no sleep, no sleep! You don't know what it's like in there, all night long things are creeping and cracking. And that red light is burning my brain!

ELAINE: You look a little stressed.

JERRY: Oh I'm stressed!

- SEINFELD, "THE CHICKEN ROASTER" EPISODE 142

// Eight hours of sleep per night?? Impossible! Heresy! Blasphemy!" Sadly, this is how most people perceive their capacity to achieve eight hours of sleep. The reality is, many jobs force us to be "always on," and that means late nights, weekends, early mornings, and less time for sleep. It's amazing that with the advances in technology geared toward increasing automation and productivity, we've paradoxically become busier, but that's the truth. Smart phones have helped enable this behavior. And we've also become dumber about how important sleep is. We brag about getting a few hours of sleep per night. We expect others to "sacrifice" like we do, and put the firm ahead of our health, or the project ahead of our sanity.

The working professional does lots of dumb things. This is one of the dumbest. You're hurting yourself, your health, your intellect, your relationships and your lifespan by sleeping so little. Nobody is going to visit your grave in 75 years and say, "what a trooper – only slept five hours per night."

This book isn't about sleep – it's about effectiveness. And nothing will kill your effectiveness more than not getting enough sleep or getting poor sleep. For those of you that have small children at home, you can ignore this section as you are in your own personal Hell that supersedes anything I am describing. But for the rest of you – listen up! This applies to you, hotshot.

Arianna Huffington is a huge champion of sleep health, especially in the professional work environment. Years ago, she was working herself to the bone as the head of "Huffington Post" until she literally collapsed due to lack of sleep. She started researching the negative effects that poor sleep habits can have on your health, and she was mortified. She couldn't believe that by not getting enough quality sleep she was putting herself in such danger.

And she realized that many working professionals – especially type A personalities – routinely neglect sleep as other priorities take over: getting that last email out, build that last report, make that one last call to the West Coast, or track down the status of a project.

In her book, *The Sleep Revolution,* she describes how you can transform your life by changing your sleep habits for the better. The gist is that you need to prioritize sleep over the work priorities that you keeping doing instead of getting some shuteye.

Studies have shown that the actions, reaction times and general awareness of a person who lacks sleep are highly correlated to that of a drunk person. So by giving up that extra few hours of sleep to answer the emails you don't really need to answer, you're turning yourself into a punch-drunk booze hound the next day. It's no way to go through life. Believe me, I know – but that's a story for another time.

You would be amazed at how much better you feel when you get a full night's sleep. You're more alert, more energized, more easily able to focus. Your health will improve, and if you're exercising, your body will feel better after getting a night to rejuvenate. You will also be in a better mood. Lack of sleep causes all sorts of unintended consequences, among them is irritability. Many times you don't even know that you're irritable, it's a subconscious state. You're in such a haze that you don't realize you're being a jerk. Don't be that jerk – get your Z's.

Important point here: if you're an insomniac, that's a totally different situation, and you can't just "sleep more." Please see your doctor about getting your insomnia under control.

DO FIRST THINGS FIRST

Steven Covey wrote the bestseller *7 Habits of Highly Effective People.* It's one of the few books that I've read multiple times. I highly recommend it – Covey was an accomplished psychologist, author, husband, father and businessman and he is erudite almost to the point of it being obnoxious. But he's such a good person you don't feel like he's being obnoxious – he was just that good of a guy.

Without spoiling the book, Covey's 7 Habits are as follows:

1. *BE PROACTIVE:* the first habit is one that I still struggle to keep, even after reading the book once in grad school and once more a few years ago. It's hard. It's so easy to be reactive, to just let the chips fall where they may. But you don't get anything done that way. The best way to approach a problem/project/opportunity is to be proactive. Ask the first question. Follow up. Do the leg work. It seems so simple, but I've found that when I'm not doing a good job at work, it's most likely because I'm not being proactive.

2. *BEGIN WITH THE END IN MIND:* you need to know what you're looking to accomplish in life. Covey has a great analogy here – a guy works his whole life climbing up the ladder, only to realize at the top that the ladder is leaning up against the wrong building.

3. *PUT FIRST THINGS FIRST:* we'll talk more about this in a minute.

4. *SEEK FIRST TO UNDERSTAND, THEN TO BE UNDERSTOOD:* without first listening to other people, you will never get them to see your side of the story. He recommends learning how to really listen – empathetic listening, he calls it. It's listening as if you were the person who's saying the words. You're not waiting for your turn to talk. It's extremely difficult to do, but you notice the difference when you do it.

5. *THINK "WIN/WIN":* this is the anti-Gordon Gekko mantra. In Wall Street, Gekko famously describes the business landscape as he sees it: "it's a zero-sum game. Somebody wins, somebody loses." Gekko is thinking in terms of scarcity. Covey thinks of

business transactions or other two-sided opportunities in terms of abundance. You can come up with creative ways for both sides to benefit from an arrangement – it's not necessary for someone to "take" the other or for one side to win and one side to lose. Done correctly, a deal is a "win" for both sides. [This may be the first time someone has contrasted Steven Covey with Gordon Gekko.]

6. **SYNERGIZE:** this is a word that was so overplayed in the late 1990's and early 2000's that it has a negative connotation now. But Covey wrote this book in 1997, before synergy became an overused term. The argument Covey makes is essentially: the whole is bigger than the sum of its parts. The previous five habits, if applied correctly, will allow you to see things in a different light, to have more creative solutions to problems, and to add more value than you could if you weren't following the other habits. If I ever get to this point, I will let you know. It sounds like Enlightenment multiplied by winning the World Series.

7. **SHARPEN THE SAW:** Covey finally relates what I believe is the most important habit. What Covey recommends is renewing yourself along the four "aspects of our nature":

   A. **PHYSICAL** – this doesn't mean deadlifting 700 pounds. But it does mean moving your body around, going for a walk, keeping active. Sitting is the new smoking.

   B. **MENTAL** – reading, writing, drawing, exercising your creativity muscles.

   C. **SOCIAL / EMOTIONAL** – service (like community activities), empathy ("seek first to understand")

D. **SPIRITUAL** – here Covey gets a little religious, which is fine, but it did turn me off slightly. His recommendation is to do some spiritual reading, like reading the Bible. He also recommends religious study and meditation. I will say that aside from the occasional prayer I throw up for a relative, I do not follow this habit at all.

Covey's book and related courses and curriculum were so successful that he wrote several other books, and he was known as an expert in personal productivity and effectiveness. His third habit: "put first things first," was so popular and important that he wrote an entirely different book about it.

In Covey's *First Things First,* he breaks down in great detail about how you can organize your tasks, your schedule / calendar, your week, and consequently your life. In this dense and technical book, he delves into details that were difficult to digest, but here is the summary.

As mentioned previously, there are 4 main quadrants of tasks in anyone's life:

- **QUADRANT 1:** Important and urgent

- **QUADRANT 2:** Important and not urgent

- **QUADRANT 3:** Not important and urgent

- **QUADRANT 4:** Not important and not urgent

You can organize your task list, or your "to do" list, very simply by bucketing each task into one of these quadrants. From there, you can further prioritize each task in its associated quadrant. Covey suggests that you arrange your tasks for the week in the four quadrants above. He recommends a weekly view because it's a realistic block of time. Daily "to do" lists can easily get too long and too cumbersome, while monthly task lists can start to look like goals and aspirations, which have the effect of demotivating you. So a week is a happy medium, where you have a list of things to accomplish and you have seven days to do it.

Once you've arranged your weekly task list into quadrants, you can prioritize what needs to get done. Covey argues that there are quadrant 1 tasks that are unavoidable, so you need to schedule those in: doctor's appointment, client meeting, finish analysis of project. Covey strongly encourages you to focus on quadrant 2 tasks: those that are not urgent but are important. He finds that these quadrant 2 tasks are the ones that are difficult, challenging, and ultimately the most personally enriching. The more time you can spend on long-term important tasks like skills development, training, practicing a new skill, or teaching, the better you'll be able to master that skill, which will further enrich your life.

Covey also mentions that quadrant 3 tasks sometimes are unavoidable but you can typically push back on these. He gives the classic argument when the boss comes up to your desk (or in your case, calls you because you're working at home) and says he has an "urgent and important" matter that needs to be attended to right away and to "drop what you're doing." You can calmly state that you are working on this other urgent, important task, and that what would he like you to drop from your already packed schedule to accommodate his urgent, "important" task? Many times the boss will realize the error of his ways and back off. I've used this strategy several times in the past, and although the boss isn't especially happy with me for employing this tactic, I remained employed after using it with no negative effects.

Covey says that quadrant 4 activities are to be avoided at all costs. He has a view of the world that anything not productive is time wasted. I tend to disagree with him, especially when it comes to quadrant 4. Sometimes I just want to sit and watch an episode of "The League." Sometimes I want to surf YouTube looking for the latest Super Training video or the one Larry Bird compilation I haven't seen yet. I may just want to doodle. I find these activities relaxing, and even if it's not "important" in accordance with my quadrants, I find it refreshing. Covey will put things like exercise, taking a walk, and meditating in quadrant 2, and I agree with him there. It makes perfect sense to build in some time for physical activity or mental acuity. I also feel that good ole fashioned loafing around, though, is something that's OK to do, too. If not, I personally get to a point where I'm feeling a bit too productive, and I go off the deep end and veg in front of the TV for a few days. "Everything in moderation," as my Mom always says.

Bottom line: Prioritize the #1's from the #3's as best you can. The quadrant 2 tasks are the sweet spot. Covey says no #4's, which I think is unreasonable, but try to limit them. I feel the quadrant 3 tasks are the worst and I avoid these at all costs.

PART 5

GET INTO THE GROOVE

M ihaly Csikszentmihalyi is a Hungarian psychologist best known as the expert on "flow," which he defines as a highly-focused mental state. I'm going to abbreviate Mihaly's name as MC in the interest of my keyboard's sanity. MC became an international phenomenon after his viral TED Talk hit the internet back in February 2004. Today it is still one of the most viewed TED Talks ever recorded.

MC argues that if you can find a problem that is difficult to solve, and you direct your attention to it, and you struggle with it, with intense focus – meaning no email interruptions, or IM's from a colleague, then eventually you will achieve flow. Flow is that mental state that for me is most comparable to "the zone" in athletics.

There was a great scene in "White Men Can't Jump" where Billy Hoyle – played by Woody Harrelson – accosts Sydney Deane – played by Wesley Snipes – and says, "you're pissed off, I'm in a zone." Deane quickly retorts, "you're not good enough to be in a zone." Being in "the zone" athletically is typically something that is reserved for elite, if not the best, athletes. Michael Jordan once made six straight three pointers against the Portland Trail Blazers in the 1992 NBA Finals. After his sixth make, he coasted backwards and threw up his hands as if to say, "hey, even I can't explain it!" Jordan was in the zone.

The zone is hard to explain. It's hard to describe, and it's hard to get into the zone. You have to be really good at what you do to get into the zone, or as the conventional wisdom goes. MC, though, argues that you can get into a flow state – a.k.a. "the zone," and that there are predictable patterns that get you into that state.

MC started his career in psychology by accident. As a young man he became intrigued with the question: what contributes to a life worth living? He read philosophy, studied the arts and other subjects, but he didn't find the answers he was looking for. One night with no money and nothing to do, he stumbled upon a presentation by Carl Jung. This was before anyone even knew who Jung was. He caught a Carl Jung lecture by chance. From there, he delved deeply into psychology and studied the idea of ecstasy, which he defines as being outside yourself with happiness. He dug deeper and discovered his now-famous concept of flow.

In his TED Talk, MC showed how several of his subjects defined flow. A poet describes it as opening a door that floats up in the sky. Einstein described something similar when he was struggling with the theory of relativity. Regardless of the discipline, the feeling of flow was similar with these top performers.

MC was able to determine based on research and interviewing these top performers that when the combination of a tough challenge and a high skill set intersect, flow is most likely to occur. So if a really good chess player is playing against another really good chess player, the odds are that one player, if not both players, will get into flow during the match.

So what does this mean for you? Hopefully you consider what you do for work a challenge - or at least some aspects of it. When you get a chance to work on a tough project, you get a little pumped up. And hopefully (for your sake) you are a skilled individual. And that doesn't mean you have to be elite or best in the world at your profession. But you have to have a level of acumen that will invite flow if the challenge is there.

I call the state that I find myself in "the groove" as opposed to "flow", but it's the same idea. Once I get my arms around a tough problem, and I have enough time to think about it, break it down, discover the real issues, and then work on a solution, I feel that flow state, that groove. Whatever you call it, get into it! You will be happy when you do – it's a state that allows you to work hard but not feel like you're working. It's almost like you're Superman.

PART 5

"HOME" CAN BE ANYWHERE SOMETIMES

'␣ve worked from "home" in Maine, Miami, New York City, Boston, Connecticut, California and Paris. I've worked from coffee shops, train stations, airports, airplanes, hotel lobbies, shared workspaces, and in the car – hands free of course.

The point is that you have tremendous flexibility as a work-at-home professional. Sometimes you spend a long weekend at your parents' house or with your wife's family. Other times you decide to hit the road early and get to the mountains to beat the crowd, and you work from the cabin. You may just want to take a quick trip to the beach. As long as the beach has wireless internet, you can do your work from the beach house or the patio.

Another option is to rent out a space really close to your home – within a short walk or less than five-minute drive. This way you're out of the house, which is especially nice if you have young children at home. And you're not in the office, so you don't have to deal with the unproductive office atmosphere. If you're a freelancer, entrepreneur, or small business owner, this is a great option. Jeff Goins, an author and successful online writing trainer, put it like this:

"What do I need to thrive in my work? I need occasional interaction with people, but often I need to be left alone to work. This was why I eventually invested in an office outside of the home, to create a separation between work life and home life."

Sometimes life gets in the way of work, and you have to take a conference call on the run, or finish up a deliverable at a coffee shop. That's' OK. It happens to all of us, and if you're lucky enough to work from home, it doesn't derail you at all.

One note of caution: do not expect to get meaningful, difficult work done in a temporary home location. That won't work – there are too many variables for distractions that you can't control. But you can mind the fort, return emails, make calls, attend meetings, and even present – although I would only do so to an internal audience. Customers don't think it's as cute when your parents' dog is barking in the background. Although Coco the cocker spaniel is a sweetheart.

PART 5

VOLUNTEER

One last thing I encourage you to do now that you have some extra time: you can volunteer. It doesn't have to be for lots of time – maybe an hour here or there. But one thing I've learned by volunteering is how much a small gesture can make a huge difference in someone else's life.

When I was working at EY in Boston, I joined the office's social responsibility team that organized various community events. One was handing out food at the local food bank. We showed up early, bagged the food into individual or family-sized packages, and handed out the food to the needy. One woman asked me to help her carry the food to her car, since she had difficulty carrying much weight. She was older and didn't walk very well.

I grabbed her food and placed it in her car for her, and she gave me a huge hug and said, "God bless you!" I wasn't expecting that, as all I did was walk a few feet with a couple bags of groceries, but she was so grateful. That has stuck with me. It's not about how much you do. Just do something. It can be small. Believe me, what seems small to you can seem really important to someone in need.

Today I make time to volunteer for a few organizations in Connecticut. I am on the foundation board of Quinebaug Valley Community College (QVCC), the local community college. We help raise money for scholarships and provide support for events throughout the year. We meet once a month, and typically it takes a little more of my time during an event. In all I spend very little time volunteering for QVCC, but the impact is felt.

I joined the QVCC board last year, and part of my responsibilities as a first-year board member was to participate in the scholarship committee.

We were split up into teams of two, and each team member read a stack of scholarship applications. We read through dozens of applications, and then the team members met to rank each student. We then took a shot at seeing which scholarship fit which student – a task similar to solving a complex puzzle. Once the teams had their rankings, the committee met to determine who got what scholarship.

In one marathon meeting, we fought it out with the other teams to pitch our students, hoping that the committee would find our selection a better fit for the scholarship than the other team's choice. This may sound competitive, and it was. No blood was drawn, but we had some contentious moments. In the end, we had selected over 100 students to receive over $100,000 in scholarship money.

Once we made our selections, it was time for Scholarship Night, where the students all received their scholarships. They knew they won something because they were invited, but they don't know how much money they were getting, and the scholarship dollar amounts vary. Some are a couple hundred dollars, and some are well over $1,000. So it can make a huge difference for these kids, especially if they win a "big prize."

As scholarship committee members, we got to hand out scholarships to the deserving students. When I saw the looks on the faces of the winners, I knew that the time I put in fighting for our team's students was worth it. It was a great feeling.

You can participate in many ways. Local organizations are always looking for help. You can volunteer at the soup kitchen, or at the local community center. You can bake some cookies for the church bake sale, or give out socks to the homeless in the city.

For me, volunteering is a way for me to remember how good I have it. I'm lucky to have been raised by good parents and have a good brother. I'm lucky I was born with a little bit of intelligence. I'm lucky I crossed paths with some of the wonderful people – mostly my wife – I have in my life. And I feel like it's the least I can do to give back. Even a little. It means so much.

PART 5

CONCLUSION

JERRY: "See now, to me, that button is in the worst possible spot."

GEORGE: "Really?"

JERRY: "Oh yeah. The second button is the key button. It literally makes or breaks the shirt. Look at it, it's too high, it's in no-man's land."

GEORGE: "Haven't we had this conversation before?"

JERRY: "You think?"

GEORGE: "I think we have."

JERRY: "Yeah, maybe we have."

- SEINFELD: THE FINALE (2), EPISODE 180

As I wrap up this book, I hope you got a sense as to how much you can accomplish by working from home. How much time you will save. How much money you will save. How much aggravation you will avoid.

Think for a moment what you would do with an extra three hours per day. Would you go to the gym? Would you take a walk? How about going to a class to learn a new skill? What about relaxing with a good book? Maybe you just want to spend some time talking with your spouse and family? Whatever you imagine, you can do with that extra time you save by not commuting to work. It's worth it for your sanity, your health, and your relationships.

In the finance world, there is an acronym called FP&A, which stands for Financial Planning & Analysis. Part of our sales pitch is that our software will let your people spend less time on the low-value P – the planning – and more time on the A – the analysis, which is a high-value activity and where you will ultimately gain insights and make progress. Think of the extra time you gain by not commuting to work as a shift in your time. You're shifting from low-value activities, like driving or sitting on a bus, to high-value activities, like exercise or spending time with your loved ones. You still get the same twenty-four hours in a day, but you can now choose to do more with those hours, without sacrificing anything, except maybe hearing a horrible joke at the water cooler.

The time savings is a huge win of working from home. But there are hard dollars you save, too: less maintenance dollars on your car, saving money on meals because you are eating home instead of on the road. That savings could be put into a savings account, or a college fund, or maybe you want to start a side business. But that additional money gives you additional options. Optionality in this world is gold. The more options you have, the better you usually make out.

Hopefully this book gave you some ideas as to what type of work you can do from home. Hopefully it also gave you a sense as to the flexibility you have as a remote worker.

My call to action if you already work at home: please share with me the types of activities or habits or methods that you use to enrich your daily work routine. You can share stories with me directly via email: **joemarkley33@gmail.com**, or you can find me on Twitter **@markleyjr.**

My call to action if you do not yet work from home: think about a way to convince your boss to work at least one day per week at home. Check in. Be Abe Lincoln. Give credit, but do it strategically. And show your boss that you can be just as effective, if not more effective, working from home. How could you not be more productive? You'll be better rested. You will probably get a chance to exercise. You can make your own food. You can concentrate, which means you have a better chance of getting into the groove. And you won't be in a bad mood because your commute sucked the life out of you.

Today's worker shouldn't have to struggle with physically getting to a cubical. It's not like you're at the textile mill and you need to work the loom. You're not standing on the assembly line at the auto plant. You're not mining coal. You're a knowledge worker, an idea person, and an intellectual. And smart people don't need to sit in traffic for a quarter of their waking hours. Let's all stop the madness, and stop the commute. And let's get to work!

BIBLIOGRAPHY

- *Secrets of Being Promoted and Earning More Money*
  COLIN SHAW
  *HTTPS://WWW.LINKEDIN.COM/PULSE/20130904124050-
  284615-SECRETS-OF-BEING-PROMOTED-AND-EARNING-MORE-
  MONEY?TRK=TOD-HOME-ART-LIST-SMALL_1*

- *Predictably Irrational*
  DAN AIERLY
  *HTTP://WWW.PRB.ORG/PUBLICATIONS/ARTICLES/2014/
  US-COMMUTING.ASPX*

- *Fortune 50 List including Merck:*
  HTTP://FORTUNE.COM/FORTUNE500/

- *Blue light causes sleep problems:*
  *HTTP://WWW.HEALTH.HARVARD.EDU/STAYING-HEALTHY/BLUE-
  LIGHT-HAS-A-DARK-SIDE*

  *HTTPS://WWW.TED.COM/TALKS/JASON_FRIED_WHY_WORK_
  DOESN_T_HAPPEN_AT_WORK?LANGUAGE=EN*

- *Seinfeld quotes:*
  HTTP://WWW.SEINFELDSCRIPTS.COM/
  HTTP://WWW.AMAZON.COM/RISE-SUPERMAN-DECODING-ULTI-
  MATE-PERFORMANCE/DP/1477800832

- *MC's Flow Ted Talk:*
  HTTPS://WWW.TED.COM/TALKS/MIHALY_CSIKSZENTMIHALYI_
  ON_FLOW#T-922405

- *Working Virtually*
  JEFF GOINS
  HTTP://GOINSWRITER.COM/VIRTUAL-WORK/

- *Oxford Study reference on what jobs will be replaced by robots:*
  HTTPS://WWW.REPLACEDBYROBOT.INFO/

ABOUT THE AUTHOR

JOE MARKLEY

J oe Markley is a software sales professional and constant tinkerer. He earned by bachelor's degree in Accounting from the University of Connecticut, and spent the first three years after graduating as a Financial Planning and Analysis (FP&A) professional and commuter. He got an MBA in Management Consulting & Finance (also from UConn), and has been working in the Enterprise Performance Management (EPM) software space since 2006.

In 2008, he was able to transition to working primarily from home, and he's been enjoying it ever since! Joe is always experimenting with better ways to get things done and still enjoy the work. If you have experiences you'd like to share with him, you can find him on Twitter **@markleyjr** or on LinkedIn at **www. linkedin.com/in/joemarkley33**. If you'd like Joe to help your organization work from home more effectively, please contact him. He'd be happy to help!